ACKNOWLEDGEMENTS

We would like to thank all the amazing Black women who took the time to share their story with authenticity, humility and kindness. Our hope is for their words to spread through the world like the fresh air we breathe in the morning. We would like to thank our sponsors, supporters, Aggie Yemurai Mutuma from Mahogany Inclusion Partners, Avanade, Firefly Communications, Marie Feliho and many more for their support in making this book a reality. We would also like to thank 3 Colours Rule Creative Agency who worked creatively with passion. Last but not least, our friends and family for always being there for us.

We thank you.

OUR MAP

Scan here to see our interactive History map!

Step into a world where history comes to life, where the threads of time weave together tales of strength, resilience, and unwavering determination. Welcome to an interactive history map that invites you on a journey through the remarkable lives of black women who defied boundaries, shattered glass ceilings, and carved their legacies across continents.

As you navigate this digital tapestry of stories, you'll discover the hidden gems of history, the stories that weren't always told in textbooks, but that resonate with power and inspiration. These are the stories of black women who, despite facing countless challenges, rose like phoenixes from the ashes of adversity to light the way for generations to come.

Imagine walking alongside a warrior queen who ruled with grace and strategy in the heart of Africa, her leadership shaping entire empires. Picture a fearless abolitionist who stood tall against the tides of injustice, her voice echoing through the corridors of time, demanding equality and freedom. Envision a scientist who unlocked the mysteries of the universe, her brilliance challenging norms and breaking barriers in the realm of exploration.

Each pinpoint on this map represents a chapter in the collective narrative of black women who dared to dream, dared to challenge, and dared to create change. Their stories are not just history, but a testament to the incredible strength that flows through the veins of their descendants. They are a reminder that even in the darkest hours, greatness can emerge, and that the shackles of the past can be shattered by the brilliance of the future.

This interactive map isn't just a digital canvas; it's a portal to empowerment. It's an opportunity to inspire the next generation, to ensure that the stories of these trailblazers are woven into the fabric of young minds. It's a chance to remind those who have been deprived of their heritage that their ancestors were not just royal and amazing, but also architects of change, visionaries of hope, and warriors of justice.

So as you journey through this map, let each story seep into your soul. Let it remind you that no dream is too big, no challenge too insurmountable. Let it fuel your passion and renew your purpose, for the stories of these extraordinary black women serve as beacons, lighting the path towards a future where equality, diversity, and inclusivity reign.

Together, let us celebrate the legacy of these incredible women and ensure that their voices, their struggles, and their triumphs are heard loud and clear. Let us carry their torch forward, illuminating the way for generations yet unborn, inspiring them to reach for the stars and to never forget the incredible tapestry of history from which they hail.

BRANDS SUPPORTING THIS BOOK

Accenture is a leading global professional services company that helps the world's leading businesses, governments and other organizations build their digital core, optimize their operations, accelerate revenue growth and enhance citizen services—creating tangible value at speed and scale.

We are a talent and innovation led company with 732,000 people serving clients in more than 120 countries. Technology is at the core of change today, and we are one of the world's leaders in helping drive that change, with strong ecosystem relationships.

We combine our strength in technology with unmatched industry experience, functional expertise and global delivery capability. We are uniquely able to deliver tangible outcomes because of our broad range of services, solutions and assets across Strategy & Consulting, Technology, Operations, Industry X and Accenture Song.

These capabilities, together with our culture of shared success and commitment to creating 360° value, enable us to help our clients succeed and build trusted, lasting relationships. We measure our success by the 360° value we create for our clients, each other, our shareholders, partners and communities.

Visit us at www.accenture.com.

Google is committed to making diversity, equity, and inclusion part of everything we do.

This commitment is reflected in both how we build our products and how we build our workforce. We're passionate about building a workforce that is representative of our users, and a workplace culture that creates a sense of belonging for everyone.

We are committed to creating meaningful change by driving race equity both in our organisation and across the wider industry. That's why we're delighted to be involved in this vital work that amplifies the voices of Black Women in Technology, to help create a future where Black girls and women can see themselves thriving and leading in the technology sector.

Goldman Sachs

At Goldman Sachs, our Engineers don't just make things – we make things possible. Build innovations that drive our business and financial markets worldwide. Solve the most challenging and pressing engineering problems for our clients. Join our engineering teams that build massively scalable software and systems, architect low latency infrastructure solutions, pro actively guard against cyber threats, and leverage machine learning alongside financial engineering to continuously turn data into action. Create new businesses, transform finance, and explore a world of opportunity at the speed of markets.

Engineering is at the critical centre of our businesses. Our dynamic environment requires strategic thinking that is innovative and produces smart solutions. Want to push the limit of digital possibilities? Start here.

For more than a century, Thales has exploited technology for the nation's benefit, developing world-leading capabilities that help our customers think smarter and act faster.

Whilst we're a global business, our footprint in the UK is both far-reaching and significant. With over 7000 people in the UK, we work across every country of the Union to help keep the nation safe and secure.

For many years, Thales in the UK has contributed to the security and stability of this nation by providing Thales groups extraordinary technology to our customers in Government and industry. Our UK operations cover all Thales' key business sectors, covering aerospace, defence, digital security, transport and space.

At Thales in the UK and globally, it is our belief that diversity and inclusion make for a stronger and more innovative workforce. For us, diversity and inclusion are embraced to foster creativity and decipher solutions to the most complex of problems. This allows us to solve some of the world's most intricate engineering challenges across an array of markets.

GTA Black Women In Tech is proud to unveil the world's first interactive historical map, chronicling the remarkable stories and profound impact of Black women towards social, economic and gender justice on a global scale. This transformative project has been realised through a collaborative partnership with UN Women Multi-Country Office (MCO)- Caribbean.

AFRICA

Scan here to learn more about Africa's history

NIGERIA

Queen Moremi (c.12th century)

Queen Moremi is a legendary figure in African history and folklore who lived in the 12th century in the Kingdom of Ife in present-day Nigeria. She was a powerful and influential queen who ruled the kingdom alongside her husband, King Oranmiyan. Despite her royal status, Queen Moremi is best known for her bravery and cunning, which helped save her people from a terrible threat.

KENYA

Grace Ogot (1930-2015)

Grace Ogot was a Kenyan author, journalist, and political figure. She was one of the first female writers from Kenya to gain international recognition, and her work often dealt with themes of gender and colonialism.

SOUTH AFRICA

Winnie Madikizela-Mandela (1936-2018)

An anti-apartheid activist and politician. She was married to former South African president Nelson Mandela for 38 years and was an iconic figure in her own right.

CHAD

Rose Lokissim (1955-1986)

Defying societal expectations, Rose shattered gender barriers, demonstrating her resolute work ethic and ambitious nature. At the age of around 23, she joined the ranks of the Chadian Army and making history as one of its pioneering female elite soldiers. When Hissène Habré officially became President of Chad in 1982, his reign turned into a dictatorship. In a chilling turn of events, anyone who dared to voice dissent faced persecution, by 1984, Rose came to a profound realisation that she could no longer be part of this. After her arrest on May 15th 1986 Rose was forcefully pulled from her confinement and was questioned. Tragically, at the young age of 31, she met her untimely demise, and was executed on the very same day.

CAMEROON

Alice Nkom (1945-present)

Alice Nkom is a Cameroonian human rights lawyer and LGBTQ rights activist. She is known for her work defending the rights of marginalised communities, particularly those of the LGBTQ community in Cameroon. Nkom has been instrumental in fighting against the criminalization of homosexuality in Cameroon and has helped many LGBTQ individuals in the country to avoid prosecution and discrimination.

FLAVILLA FONGANG

FOUNDER OF GTA BLACK WOMEN IN TECH

In the intricate tapestry of my life, the threads of history, identity, and destiny are interwoven in a captivating narrative that unfolds across continents and generations. Born in the radiant land of France, a place where history courses through every cobblestone, I embarked on a journey of self-discovery that would forever alter my perception of self and illuminate the legacy that courses through my veins.

In the shadows of time, Cameroon stands as a testament to the colonial clash of empires—French, English, and German—a country marked by the indelible imprints of European dominion. It's here, amidst the echoes of a rich and complex past, that my journey begins.

As a young girl, sitting in the classroom, I was taught the stories of France, the annals of its triumphs and tribulations. Yet, I was left with a lingering curiosity about my own name, Fongang. A name that felt like a puzzle piece misplaced, a riddle whose answer lay shrouded in history's enigma. I held the assumption that it might be tied to the painful legacy of a slave master, a weighty inheritance to bear.

However, it was a single conversation with my father that became the catalyst for an odyssey of enlightenment. With his gentle encouragement, I embarked on a voyage of ancestral exploration. Through the labyrinth of research and discovery, I uncovered the truth behind the name Fongang—a name steeped in resilience, strength, and defiance.

Their odyssey led them from the clutches of Egyptian captivity to the expanse of In the heart of Central Africa, the Fongang legacy sprang forth from the lineage of black Hebrews who dared to defy oppression. Cameroon, a land often referred to as the "small Africa" due to its diverse array of tribes. My great-grandfather, a beacon of leadership and power, reigned as king over one of these tribes, commanding vast swathes of land that resonated with their ancestral stories.

And so, my father, the prince of our ancestral realm, bequeathed to me a lineage that was a symphony of sovereignty and strength. The realisation of my royal heritage was a revelation that shattered the walls of self-doubt and infused my spirit with newfound pride. Armed with the knowledge of my forebears, I embarked on a journey to a city where cultures converged and dreams, London.

As I stepped into the realm of entrepreneurship, I carried with me not just the weight of my name, but the legacy of warriors and rulers. The legacy of high standards, unyielding excellence, and regal poise had been passed down through generations.

Every endeavour I pursued, every partnership I forged, was imbued with the essence of my heritage—a heritage that spoke to me of courage, audacity, and the pursuit of greatness. The legacy of Fongang was not merely a name; it was a declaration of strength, an anthem of perseverance, and a crown of regality.

My story is a testament to the power of embracing one's history. As you embark on your own journey, remember this: Embrace your heritage, cherish your legacy, and with your head held high, stride confidently into the world, for you are the living embodiment of a history that is as extraordinary as it is enduring.

> **" Embrace your heritage, cherish your legacy. "**

Scan here to learn
more about Flavilla

CONTENTS

WHY 51 STORIES?

Equality is what the world needs. So a little more should be done to readjust the balance of opportunities.

_____

AISHA JUSTIN

SOFTWARE ENGINEER, AMERICAN EXPRESS

How a 'Gucci' Computer Launched My Career in Tech: I was six years old and living in Zimbabwe when I followed my mother to work one day, and the computer science teacher allowed me to sit and use his computer. I played Minesweeper and it was from that moment I decided I wanted to work with computers when I grew up. I've never looked back since. Unfortunately, I did not get another chance to touch a computer until many years later.

When I turned 10, my family relocated to South Africa. The move was a big one. Starting high school in a new country while not speaking English and the many languages of South Africa, I mostly felt out of place.

In year 10, I took up Information Technology as a subject and fell in love with the Delphi programming language. Although my entire sophomore class was new to Delphi, our teacher pushed us all to build projects and enrolled us into IT competitions. My first winning project was from Year 11 with a company named Embarcadero. When my parents were invited to come and see my work, they noticed that other children had laptops and I did not – this made them feel embarrassed. As soon as they left the school, they went to the mall and bought me the best laptop they could find. I named that laptop 'Gucci' and Gucci quickly became my family's most prized treasure. With Gucci, I felt invincible, and my family supported my passion for tech.

After high school, I took a two-year IT internship. In that same period, I failed my Java Oracle Exams three times. I was not deterred. I applied to the University of Johannesburg in South Africa to study Computer Science and Informatics.

At university, I was introduced to new programming languages such as C#, C++, PHP, and Python. I did a lot of self-learning and therefore was able to pick up things very fast and I started working part-time at several companies as a web developer. Then I discovered hackathons and hacks became my new hobby.

In 2019 I came across the GirlCode hackathon in South Africa sponsored by Amex. I came out in 2nd place and a week after the hack, I received a phone call, and I was offered a place on the Amex Technology Graduate Program in the UK. I scored a permanent role shortly after. I currently work on a very supportive team where I feel valued and positive about my career growth.

Lately, I have been exploring work with Docker, Kubernetes, APIs and learning as much as I can. I love getting involved in community projects that expose children to tech and encourage more females to take up a career in IT.

If I could write a letter to my children or grandchildren, I would tell them, "Do not be afraid to clear your throat and speak up. Anything and everything is already yours - go for it with confidence."

"

Anything &
everything
is yours - go
for it with
confidence.

"

Scan here to learn
more about Aisha

AKOSUA KUDOM

MANAGEMENT CONSULTANT, ACCENTURE

I was born in Ghana and spent my early years in an area known fondly as "Oxford Street", so it was inevitable that I would love the city. At five, I moved to southeast London with my two younger sisters.

After less than a year in a council house in West Norwood, my family moved to a council house in Crystal Palace. My mum worked multiple jobs and still managed to find time to take me and my sisters out. This, along with the importance my mum placed on listening to us read, complete our homework, tell creative stories, and pray morning and night, taught me the power of learning, stories and believing in a God greater than yourself.

I loved school, but there was one thing I struggled with. I would sometimes be teased by the other children about my Ghanaian accent, so I learned to stay quiet, even if that wasn't who I was. I had a best friend who was very loud, popular, and chatty, but rarely knew the answers to questions in class. I would whisper the answers to her, and she would very proudly and loudly share them with the class. It was a great partnership. I learned the value of teamwork and combining our strengths.

I later went to a girls' state school that specialised in science and technology where I found my voice. Everywhere I looked, young girls were in science labs doing experiments with Bunsen burners, in our sports field, and doing craft, design and technology. Our school walls were plastered with images and stories of eminent women such as Ada Lovelace, Marie Curie, and Harriet Tubman.

I loved science, art and technology and knew that I wanted to combine my love for all three.

Leading Accenture's cloud agenda for our Talent and Organisation practice gives me the opportunity to combine everything I love. I get to help clients solve problems, creating opportunities to help their businesses, people, and society. Beyond the partnership with clients, I enjoy contributing to marketing the purpose of Accenture's African Caribbean network, co-founding our Strategy & Consulting advocacy programme to promote the development and progression of Black and other under-represented groups.

I'm grateful for all the amazing people I continue to learn from at Accenture, including the inspiring progression and coaching from Sevasti Wong to our T&O leaders. I'm also incredibly grateful to the Cloud First and CMT teams. I feel so lucky to learn from the amazing Black leaders we have at Accenture, such as Ugo Ojike, Gavin Young, Barry Elbashir, Kysha Gibson, Elom Tay, Andy Tay, and Chloe Leonard.

I'm excited every day to have the opportunity to contribute to Accenture's mission of delivering on the promise of technology and human ingenuity. I would encourage anyone with a passion for people and technology to go for it, it's an exciting time to be in tech and the possibilities are endless. Don't be put off by being the only one or one of a few. There's power of being a pioneer so embrace the opportunity to forge the way for others.

The industry eagerly awaits your brilliance.

Scan here to learn more about Akosua

AMARACHI OKEREKE

SERVICE DELIVERY ANALYST, CAPGEMINI

For many women, their working dream died when they started having kids. I am a firm believer in the phrase 'you can have it all'. Family, money, love, good life, and health. Nothing should ever stop your dream. My mum remained illiterate because she couldn't balance being a mum and going to school. She had to drop out, something she still regrets today.

I was born in Nigeria, the third daughter and fourth child in a family of seven. Growing up was tough. My parents were both petty traders who did not earn much.

In school, I struggled badly with the Sciences, and Mathematics was my worst enemy. I hated that subject so much that the mere thought of it gave me the shivers, so I decided STEM was not for me. At University, I studied English Language and Literature and at the end of my studies, I became a teacher.

Teaching was one of the best things that happened to me. It taught me resilience, discipline, and patience. It gave me the confidence to challenge myself and the power to believe I can do anything.

After I got married and moved to the UK. I did my research and did not need a soothsayer to tell me that teaching in the UK was not for me. I was ready to take on new challenges and move into a career that would afford me more flexibility. As a mum with four little children, I knew it was not going to be easy juggling work and family, so carefully considered my next career choice.

I heard about a career fair and attended. It was all about programming, initially I thought I must have been in the wrong space. What business did I have with scientific computer programming? I decided to give it a go. If I can be a teacher, then I can learn anything.

While transitioning into tech may have looked effortless from the outside, doing it as mum with four little kids was one of the toughest things I have ever done. With no direction and lack of funds, I started my journey. I did the Harvard CS50 – Introduction to Computer Science course and later proceeded to learning how to code myself through free online materials.

While studying, I hit rock bottom with JavaScript. It became another Mathematics blocker. Though it was tough, I became tougher!

My breakthrough finally came when I discovered 'CodeYourFuture', an organisation that helps people from disadvantaged backgrounds learn coding for free. I enrolled in their eight months intensive course, became a Software Engineer and landed my first tech job in the best tech company before graduation. I did it!

For once I felt seen, I didn't give up on my dream, and I didn't quit like my mum. If I can do it with four little children, then you can. Never limit yourself or think it's too late. Always remember that your wings already exist all you need is to fly. Let nothing stop you.

" Your wings already exist, all you need is to fly. "

Scan here to learn more about Amarachi

ANDREA ASAMOAH

SENIOR SOFTWARE ENGINEER, AMERICAN EXPRESS

By the age of 7, I thought I had it all planned. I really liked my teacher at school, so I decided: 'become a teacher'. This is not exactly where I am today but seeing a role I aspired to be, has stayed with me...

From a young age, I liked playing computer games with my sisters. I remember playing one particular racing game, where I was terrible at driving so instead, I drove the reverse way of the track. This was not the traditional way but over time it helped me learn how to drive the right way. Overcoming challenges like this was one of my first loves of using computers.

My parents always encouraged my sisters and I to work hard and be the 'best'. They shared stories of life growing up in Ghana and encouraged us to put 100% into whatever we did. During secondary school, I was drawn to the logic in Mathematics, as well as IT. I also liked finding ways to share my knowledge, so I volunteered in homework and reading clubs. I was later selected to be part of a development programme with the Windsor Fellowship that helped under-represented people reach their full potential. This was a fantastic opportunity to meet others like me. It gave me the confidence to seek bigger opportunities, including summer internships at global companies during the school holidays, and later on whilst at university.

Speaking of university, I knew early on that I wanted to go, but I was worried about making the wrong decision. I realised Computer Science was an option but it wasn't a popular choice for women but I still felt that it could bring my love of Mathematics and IT together.

During the first year of my degree, some of my peers had been coding for years and seemed to already know what they were doing. I had just started coding and felt intimidated but support from my family helped and over time I found my rhythm. I still enjoyed teaching and mentoring, so I also did the Undergraduate Ambassadors scheme, working as a teaching assistant in a secondary school.

Following my degree, I completed a graduate programme in an investment bank. The different rotations in project management, coding and support helped me decide that I wanted to focus on coding. The majority of my roles thereafter have been a hybrid of technical support/analysis and coding in the financial and healthcare industries. One constant I have maintained is continuing to share my knowledge and experience through mentoring and leadership, which provides me with a real sense of reward and satisfaction. Combining my passion for helping and teaching others with creating software wasn't an obvious path. It looks different to what I originally imagined but this has evolved from me following what I enjoy and shaping my own journey.

If I could speak to my younger self, I would say...
You don't need to have everything figured out. Failure is part of learning. It's not always about the end result, enjoy the journey!

"

It's not always about the end result, enjoy the journey!

"

Scan here to learn more about Andrea

ANGIE MADARA

FOUNDING PARTNER, ATHENA FUNDX

Empowering Black Women in Tech Entrepreneurship: My Journey of Resilience and Impact

As the youngest of six children, I grew up in Kenya under the unwavering support of my incredible mother. Our family of eight resided in a small two-bedroom council house, and my mother's determination knew no bounds. She worked tirelessly, was in perpetual debt and sacrificed everything to provide us with the best private education available. Witnessing her sacrifices, I realized that I had no excuse to slack off.

My journey into tech entrepreneurship began during my undergraduate years when I founded a HealthTech startup. Supported by my university and later receiving funding from the Gates Foundation, we made significant progress. However, my second venture in people tech brought harsh realities to the forefront. We were ill-prepared to face the lack of support and the absence of a robust go-to-market strategy, leading to its eventual failure. Seeking to refine my skills, I ventured into the corporate world, gaining invaluable experience across 18 countries and reigniting my passion for product development.

Inspired by this passion, I established my third startup; an EdTech venture that merged play with key academic concepts. After successfully exiting that endeavor, I became driven to empower more women and girls to pursue tech entrepreneurship. This drive led to the creation of Athena FundX, an organization committed to fostering inclusivity through our "1 Million Women in Tech Entrepreneurship" campaign. As a woman of color, I faced inherent disadvantages in an industry that often favors those who fit within traditional power structures.

Yet, I refuse to let these challenges define me.

Instead, I have transformed them into motivation to challenge the status quo and create a platform that empowers women of color in entrepreneurship. Now, as a mother of two wonderful, inquisitive girls who share a passion for technology and building things, I feel compelled to ensure that future generations of black girls can actualize their dreams.

To aspiring black female tech entrepreneurs and other black women in tech, I offer the following advice:

Believe in yourself: Embrace your abilities and have confidence in your unique perspective and talents. You possess the power to achieve greatness.

Embrace failure: Failure is not an endpoint but a stepping stone on the path to success. Learn from setbacks, adapt, and keep pushing forward.

Seek opportunities for growth: Never stop learning. Foster diversity and inclusion: Use your platform to uplift and empower others. Create opportunities for underrepresented groups, amplifying their voices and driving positive change.

By embracing our individual journeys, surmounting challenges, and fostering inclusion, we can inspire a new generation of black women in tech and reshape the industry. Together, we will create a future where diversity and innovation thrive, breaking down barriers and unleashing the full potential of black women in the tech world.

Let us rise, empower, & lead the way.

Scan here to learn more about Angie

ANTONIA DOUGLAS

CYBER SECURITY ASSURANCE LEAD,
INTERNATIONAL AIRLINES GROUP

Embarking on a journey in the tech industry wasn't originally a life objective, yet my dyslexia altered the course of my life's path. Failing my A-levels due to the challenges posed by dyslexia could have been disheartening, but instead, it became my turning point in the dynamic realm of the tech industry. Recognizing my affinity for technology during an IT BTEC course, I uncovered a passion that transcended the conventional classroom barriers. Unlike traditional academic paths, the tech world valued problem-solving, innovation, and diverse thinking – qualities that aligned with my unique perspective shaped by dyslexia. This realization ignited a fire within me to harness my differences as strengths, propelling me toward a career where creativity, adaptability, and determination were prized assets. Embracing technology not only empowered me to overcome setbacks but also enabled me to thrive in an environment that celebrated my distinctive abilities and fostered my growth as a tech enthusiast.

Discovering that I had dyslexia was a relief, but I knew the road ahead wouldn't be without its challenges. Undeterred, I persisted, and I proudly graduated with a degree in Computing and Management. Early in my professional journey, I grappled with the fear of rejection when applying for internships and graduate programs. I persisted, and as a part of my sandwich degree, I secured a one-year IT internship. Upon leaving university I was awarded a place on a two-year technology graduate scheme.

Entering the corporate world marked a distinct shift from academia, where my differences weren't always embraced. Unlike my university experience, which provided essential support, I felt the need to forego assistance as a working professional.

Concealing my disability became a protective shield, allowing me to blend in and avoid scrutiny. I didn't want to acknowledge what I perceived as a weakness needing reasonable accommodations.

Advocating for a better understanding of dyslexia and dispelling misconceptions is paramount. As a member of the neuro-diverse community, I recognize that while I may be different, I share a bond with those who possess similar exceptional skills. Dyslexia doesn't hinder me from taking on challenges; rather, it pushes me to work twice as hard to achieve my goals.

Currently, I work as a cybersecurity expert, having previously served as a network security analyst and a risk manager, and now holding the position of an assurance lead. Being neurodiverse with dyslexia, I deeply appreciate the significance of tailored support for achieving success. While my primary focus lies in the field of cybersecurity, I am also a passionate advocate for inclusivity. I find great fulfilment in mentoring and providing assistance to individuals facing neurodiversity challenges.

> ## I share a bond with those who possess similar exceptional skills.

Scan here to learn more about Antonia

AURÉLIE CORIDON

EXPERIENCE TRANSFORMATION MANAGER, ACCENTURE

I am an ambitious and highly determined individual who stems from a family composed of members from the far-reaching corners of the world, which has shaped my adaptability to different environments and groups of people.

Born and raised in France to Caribbean parents, I was generally sheltered from the racism that other first and second-generation French people from minority communities often feel. However, I can recall an early confrontation with the ugly face of prejudice at the age of five while visiting Spain. Another little girl made the remark of being unable to play with me due to my skin colour. Innocent in my response, I said, "I'm not too black, I'm brown". I could not understand why another person would highlight something she never felt differentiated her from another human being. Moving on from school, I studied advertising and communications. With an interest in creativity and mass media strengthened with my first degree, I wanted to focus more on data and digital marketing, meaning that I embarked on a master's degree in digital marketing in Lille.

Following graduation, I landed my first job in Montreux, managing a retail company's website. Although the role was highly fulfilling, my strive to challenge myself led to my decision to relocate to the United Kingdom. Although the move was initially temporary, I fell in love with London's vibrancy and fast paced nature along with the career opportunities it presented. I am now a Manager in Engagement and Activation at Accenture Song. I create relevant communication experiences that deliver a mutually beneficial connection for both brand and customer. This primarily involves using customer knowledge to design how, where and when to best reach them, and using this information to implement and manage optimal communication campaigns to deliver this valued exchange.

Away from work, I am a mother to a 6-year-old son, balancing personal and professional demands. As one can imagine, raising a young male in today's urban environment can be very challenging, presenting many dangers from exposure to prejudices and violence that make me very passionate about advocating for speaking up in the face of injustices and recognising self-worth for those with disadvantages. Whether it be these challenges or adapting to life in a foreign country during a global pandemic with no family close by to support, I have endured all of life's challenges, but I haven't done it alone, or without the amazing support and flexibility at Accenture. I am forever grateful to my mentor Peru Fourie and managers Kwesi Twerefoo and Helen Russell.

Looking towards the future, I am continually developing my expertise around CRM, marketing, data and customer experience. I want to continue to be an excellent role model to my son and an inspiration to other Black women. I hope that I can show that anything is achievable with the right mindset and determination. The world is changing, and you can be the first to break the barriers for those that come after you to make our world more inclusive, more colourful, more diverse. Do not be afraid of being the only one that looks like you in the room, do not be intimidated and know you have every right to belong in every space. Differences are to be embraced, whether it be a different accent, hairstyle or background. The world is your oyster and we all set the example for the future.

"

The world is
your oyster,
we all set an
example for
the future.

"

Scan here to learn
more about
Aurelie

BAMIDELE FARINRE

PATHOLOGY QUALITY MANAGER/ GOVERANCE LEAD/ CERTIFIED SCRUM MASTER, WHITTINGTON NHS

My name is Bamidele Farinre, and I hail from Nigeria, where I spent my early years until my teenage years. During my adolescence, I relocated to the UK to join my parents and siblings. The name "Bamidele" originates from the Yoruba ethnic group and language in Nigeria. It carries significant meaning, which can be interpreted as "follow me home" or "follow me to prosperity." This name embodies qualities of leadership, guidance, and the ability to bring joy and good fortune to others. My married name, Farinre, holds its own unique significance, suggesting the potential and capacity to achieve great things becoming trailblazers in their chosen fields.

I grew up in Southeast London on a council estate, surrounded by hardworking parents with diverse occupations. My father works as a bus driver, while my mother is a retired homemaker. During my childhood, I aspired to become a pharmacist, inspired by the life-saving impact of medicine prescriptions, particularly for those who lacked access in my community.

However, I faced my first setback at the age of 17 when I didn't succeed in my A-level exams. At that time, my lecturer discouraged me from considering a resit, suggesting that I lacked the aptitude for academic pursuits. Although this news devastated me, it didn't deter my determination. I enrolled in another college, where I triumphantly passed my A-levels. This achievement allowed me to pursue HND Applied Biology and ultimately embark on a degree in Biomedical Science.

The experiences of my childhood taught me the values of prudence, resilience, and compassion, adapting to a new culture, education, and way of life.

However, carving out my career path, I encountered obstacles due to my parents' unfamiliarity with the UK's education/career systems. To aid our adjustment, my father registered my siblings and me in community clubs, providing opportunities to partake in trips, competitions, and cultural enrichment.

Growing up in a community that fostered learning and personal growth has profoundly influenced my development. At the age of 16, I commenced working with young adults who had learning disabilities, which allowed me to tap into my innate caring and empathetic nature.

In my career journey, I have achieved remarkable milestones, taking immense pride in my accomplishments as a chartered scientist and certified scrum master, along with holding significant responsibilities in various esteemed positions. These include serving as the deputy chair of the Institute of Biomedical Sciences Virology Specialist SAP and an active member of their congress planning committee. Additionally, I contribute as an HCPC Registration assessor, serving as a school governor, and acting as a role model for the WISE campaign's 'My Skills My Life'. Moreover, I am an Inspiring the Future STEM ambassador, IBMS Mentor, Freedom to Speak Up ambassador, British Science Association Crest award assessor, and IBMS CPD officer. In these diverse roles, my utmost commitment lies in fostering inclusion and diversity, striving to amplify the voices of my colleagues and advocate for the future generation of women leaders in my community.

> "In the middle of difficulty lies opportunity.
> - Albert Einstein"

Scan here to learn more about Bamidele

BERNADINE PIERRE

SOFTWARE DEVELOPER, HOWDEN GROUP HOLDINGS

In the face of many challenges, I was determined to enter the technical field, and I made it happen.

During the pandemic, in the summer of 2021, I moved from the US to the UK to be with my partner. It was a difficult decision because my visa was about to expire, so I had only one month to pack up and start a new life in a different country. What do I pack in two suitcases? What are the people like? Will I adjust to the weather!? So many questions and concerns and so little time. I felt overwhelmed, to say the least. However, I viewed this as an opportunity for personal growth and focused on transitioning into the tech industry.

I faced a lot of rejection looking for work, not only because I had little to no tech experience, but also because I was not a UK/EU citizen or a permanent resident, which disqualified me from many programmes and opportunities. It was discouraging getting excited at a new job post or placement and then reading the eligibility requirements that automatically ruled you out. In life and many spaces, I have been ruled out and overlooked simply because of my appearance or demeanor (Black, women, introverted, etc.), and now I had to add immigration status to the list.

However, I did not let the constant rejection stop me. I took any technical course that would accept me and improved my skills through online IT courses and web development programmes. I also attended in-person events (that were allowed at the time), and I was very intentional about promoting my online profile and networking.

After six months of hard work, networking, and resourcefulness, I landed a Software Development Apprenticeship. I am still in that role and have recently been promoted! I enjoy my work and now give back by volunteering and supporting the organisations that gave me a chance. Although my journey in tech has just begun, I have already helped many young people develop their skills to break into the industry.

We have all witnessed enough struggles in our lives; it is time to balance that out with the stories of success. Representation matters, and seeing someone who looks like you triumph over adversity can be transformative. This is why I want to share my story - to empower Black women and girls and to show that you have a place to thrive professionally.

As a Black woman, I understand the importance of creating spaces where we can succeed in industries that have been dominated by others. My story is a testament to the fact that with determination, continuous learning, and belief, you can achieve your dreams in the tech industry and beyond. Let's break through the limitations set by society. Together, we can inspire and uplift one another, leaving a lasting impact on the world.

Together, we can inspire & uplift one another.

Scan here to learn more about Bernadine

EUROPE

Scan here to
learn more about
Europe's history

ENGLAND

Una Marson (1905-1965)

In 1932, Marson moved from Jamaica to London and became involved in the British feminist and anti-colonial movements. She was a leading voice for women's rights and wrote for various newspapers and magazines. She was also a frequent contributor to BBC Radio and was the first black woman to be employed by the BBC in 1935. During her time at the BBC, Marson was a pioneer in promoting the work of black writers and musicians, and was a strong advocate for the rights of women and people of colour.

SWITZERLAND

Tilo Frey (1923-2008)

A Swiss politician, who made history as the first person of African descent and one of the first women to be elected to the National Council in Switzerland. She joined the Free Democratic Party of Switzerland (FDP), and in 1964 she won a seat in Neuchâtel's city council. She was elected to the National Council in 1971, where she served for 20 years.

NORWAY

Ruth Reese (1921-1990)

A trailblazer in the Norwegian music industry. She was one of the first prominent black singers in Norway and paved the way for future generations of musicians. She was also a strong advocate for racial equality and used her platform to bring attention to the issues of discrimination and prejudice in Norway. Her work inspired countless young musicians and encouraged a new generation of artists to pursue their passions and dreams, regardless of their race or background.

FRANCE

Josephine Baker (1906-1975)

She was an American-born French dancer, singer, and actress who rose to fame in the 1920s and 1930s as a performer in France. Throughout her career, Baker used her platform to fight for civil rights and equality. She was a member of the French Resistance during World War II, and her performances often had political undertones that addressed the fight for equal rights and freedom.

CATIA BARBOSA QUETA

SENIOR DATA ANALYST, PEARSON

I often say that I would not be here today if it were not for my mother. She has shaped me into the woman I am today. My mother is a determined, hardworking person who is always striving to provide the best opportunities for me. She worked tirelessly to ensure I could follow my dreams of going to university. Her unwavering dedication and sacrifices towards my education and well-being inspired me to push myself and never take any opportunity for granted.

I grew up in a modest household where every financial decision carried great weight because there was not much to go round. My parents invested in tutors to boost my academic performance, recognizing the importance of education in opening doors for me. My mother always ensured I had decent clothes and could present myself with confidence due to fear of no one not taking me seriously. The scarcity of resources limited my choices, and I felt a sense of obligation to follow the prescribed path of success, rather than exploring my own desires and passions.

Throughout my life, I lived with the pressure to excel, and to never disappoint my family. The fear of failure weighed heavily on me, driving me to strive for perfection in everything I did. This mindset often hindered my ability to take risks or step out of my comfort zone. Over time, however, I realised that failure is not synonymous with disappointment. It is through failure that we learn, grow, and ultimately achieve greater success.

Embracing this shift in perspective has allowed me to embrace challenges and explore new opportunities without the paralysing fear of failure.

Reflecting on my accomplishments, I take pride in being the first among my cousins to attend university and the first in my family to obtain a master's degree. These milestones signify not only personal achievements but also the progress my family has made.

Additionally, I have advanced in my career and now hold a senior position within my company. This growth has been fueled by my thirst for knowledge, as well as the invaluable support and guidance from my mother. She taught me how to navigate the world and never lose my principles as a black woman.

Looking ahead, my focus is on pursuing my own aspirations and creating a meaningful impact. One of my new goals is to develop my own website, a platform that showcases data insights to people. I want to use my expertise and passion for analytics to make information accessible and empower others to make informed decisions. It's a step towards aligning my professional endeavours with my personal interests, and I am excited to embark on this new journey.

My family's sacrifices and unwavering support have shaped my values and driven me to achieve significant milestones. The constraints of limited financial resources instilled in me a strong work ethic and a commitment to success. Over the years, I have evolved, recognizing that failure is not the end but rather a stepping stone to growth.

If I could speak to my younger self, I would say...
To never be afraid to ask questions. The knowledge you gain along the way will contribute towards your development. That is how you became the best one out there in the field.

Never be
afraid to ask
questions.

Scan here to learn
more about Catia

CHELSEA MAFFIA

FOUNDER & CEO, PLAY MORGAN STUDIOS

Raised in Brixton, South London, known for its high-crime and poverty. My childhood was filled with gang culture and instability. Surrounded by a predominantly white family and spending most of my time without my parents, I constantly felt 'rootless' and misplaced; however, I always knew there was much more to life.

I spent a lot of time watching TV programs such as 'Revenge', which gave me an outlook on life that was opposite of my reality, showing safety, stability and success. Fueling my desire to achieve.

Having spent 13 years in the concrete jungle of London, I was sent to secondary school in Kent. I spent the next 4-years battling with racism, bullying and isolation which fuelled the need to take control and ownership of my life.

Finishing school on a Tuesday in May, I started an apprenticeship in Property Management on Thursday. The fun of my apprenticeship dwindled fast, being under 18 I wasn't legally allowed to do majority of the duties I was given. It then came to a complete end when I had £300 stolen from my purse by a coworker.

Knowing there was more to be done, I applied for an evening course as a mature applicant (at 17) at Greenwich University. Working from 8pm - 5pm at my estate agency job and taking class from 6pm - 9pm grinded through the next 3 years to achieve my degree in Business.

The 8-years that followed saw me through 22 jobs in various sectors, you name it - I've done it! None lasted long - none felt... right.

In 2019 while traveling through Asia I found out I was expecting a baby! A miracle, that I was told, could be medically impossible. Confused, shocked but mostly overjoyed.

During my pregnancy fear sparked - that through lack of opportunity my son would fall victim to my most dreaded stereotype, that of a young black boy growing up in South London. The fear and deep rooted purpose led me to found Play Morgan Studios - my EdTech startup; focused on the gamification and simplification of education. A company that makes learning presumably hard to attain skills easy, accessible and affordable in order to open up the landscape of opportunities for people that need it most.

Since launch, my business has grown exponentially within less than a year of launch, we have impacted 5000 lives across 82 countries, raised funds, been nominated for awards and continue to grow day by day.

To all black women please remember, your potential knows no bounds. YOU have the ability to open the doors to any industry YOU choose. The time to step into your power is now. Let your presence be a testament to the change you wish to see in the world. Embrace the opportunities, challenges, and possibilities that lie ahead, for they are all part of your unique journey as a black woman. Your voice matters, your vision matters, and your impact can reshape the future. Live in your power and let your light shine brightly.

"

Live in
your power
& let your
light shine
brightly.

"

Scan here to learn
more about
Chelsea

CHENELLE ANSAH

GENERAL PARTNER, LIGHTPACE VC

My name is Chenelle Ansah and I am one of a few Black women at Partner level in Venture Capital in the UK. I am on a personal mission to change this. There should be more of us!

I am the firstborn to a working-class Ghanaian family. Statistics say that I should not be where I am in life today, but it's important to defy the odds. I recently met an old friend who asked, "what made you make the choices you've made in life and attain your achievements?". My response was 'there has always been a niggling voice inside of me that said you can do better and so I did. I've listened to that voice my whole life and it's led me to achieve great things.

When I was young I was very much a creative, I used to teach dance and studied textiles and fashion. The agreement between me and my parents was that I could study fashion as long as I kept up my A-level grades in Business, Economics and IT and I didn't. I did terribly in my exams and failed because I spent most of my time dreaming about becoming a fashion designer.

I then dropped fashion and ended up focusing on Business Management in College and then Business Management and Accounting at Brunel University on an excellence scholarship. Despite my creative youth and dreams of becoming a fashion designer, I was very interested in business and entrepreneurship and more importantly 'making money'. During my degree at university, I took a gap year and landed a job at Society General's Investment Bank and graduated two years later and ended up in a similar role.

I didn't last very long as an Investment Banker as I didn't enjoy it and switched to being a Management Consultant selling Tech and delivering digital transformation programmes. I chose this career because I enjoyed problem solving, working in teams?

This was an amazing role for a young woman in her 20s, as I had the opportunity to travel around the world. In 2017 I decided to open my consultancy, Nell consulting, specialising in building digital banks that were Venture Capital backed. Whilst I enjoyed the work that I was doing, it became apparent that I was often the only Black woman in the room and for me this had to change. I then joined Cornerstone Partners, the UK's first Black owned investment firm investing in early-stage tech companies owned by Black and Diverse teams.

My role as a Partner and the Head of Cornerstone Partners was the start of my adventure into the world of Venture Capital, but more importantly it opened my eyes to the disparity and inequity in the industry.

The industry of Venture Capital has been considered to be somewhat elite and inaccessible. The jobs are not advertised, and we were not taught about this industry in school. In 2020 a report produced by Extend Ventures published that only 0.24% of venture capital funding went to black-owned start-ups and of this, 0.02% went to black women. This needs to change and the only way that this will change is if there are more Black women writing cheques.

If I could speak to my younger self I would say... Don't be afraid to take up space and shine. Do not minimise yourself to make others feel confident. Shine, because it's your God-given right to do so!

Don't be
afraid to
take up
space &
shine.

Scan here to
learn more about
Chenelle

CHIBBY DANGANA

LEAD, DATA & ANALYTICS (RISK & CONTROLS), NATWEST GROUP

"DO IT AFRAID"

I've always referred to myself as 'Happy-go-lucky', I grew up in a middle income household in Nigeria, Africa, I was the last of four (4) children, three boys and myself, so it would be no surprise that I was referred to as a "tomboy" growing up. Memories of my childhood are exciting ones of me staging plays with the neighbors, playing football with my brothers and friends etc. and some not so exciting ones of me helping my mum out in the kitchen even when I didn't feel like it. My mother was a Secretary/Administrator at the time for one of the Federal Aviation Institutions in Nigeria but she had a small business as a caterer, which seemed cool because our house was always stuffed with food, cake, pastries etc.

I attended primary and junior secondary schools close to the house and enjoyed walking to school with friends in the neighborhood. In senior secondary, my mum preferred that I went to a girls only boarding school, and that kicked off my journey to independence. It was the first time I was leaving my house all by myself and I cried every single day for the first month away from home. I was a really skinny girl with scampi natural hair and I wasn't very confident in my looks. I always admired the girls with nice long hair and asked God why my story was different (LOL).

As I transitioned from secondary school to University, I studied Mathematics & Statistics at the University of Lagos, Nigeria (UNILAG). I actually enjoyed Mathematics because my Dad invested time tutoring me at home from a young age. I knew I had a knack for analytical thinking and I loved computers, post graduation from University, I got my first job as an IT Project

Officer, about 8 hours from home and so I had to relocate and lived with my cousin for a few years before I got married in 2008 and went on to have 2 beautiful kids - Daniella (15) and Isaiah (12).

My career in Data Management and Health Systems Strengthening opened doors for me Nationally, I supported the Federal Ministry of Health in Nigeria in strengthening their Data & Reporting. This opportunity became the door opener to the United Kingdom in 2019 when the British Government opened its doors to Exceptional Talents in Technology Globally, like i said before - I applied afraid, but each time I was bold enough to take a step, a little voice within me always whispered "Chibby, you've got this!".

In 2023, I'm super proud of my accomplishments - Leading Data Analytics in Risk & Controls at Natwest Bank, Founder of Reeach, a thriving social enterprising supporting ethnic minorities integrate seamlessly in the United Kingdom and just recently launched a Made in Africa fashion e-commerce store called CeeDee's, and do i need to say that the timid, shy girl doesn't exist anymore? As you push yourself to dream, to believe in that little voice within you, to keep accomplishing your goals with excellence, the world is definitely your oyster.

> " Push yourself to dream, believe in that little voice within you. "

Scan here to learn more about Chibby

CHINAZOR VIVIAN KALU

PROGRAM MANAGER, NIYO GROUP

Growing up in Eastern Nigeria during a time when the worth of a girl child was overlooked, I witnessed my father's determination to defy societal expectations. He believed that a girl's destiny was not limited to the confines of the kitchen. Despite earning a meagre salary as a humble servant, he worked tirelessly to support my mother's education. Today, my mother holds a PhD, has travelled extensively, and is a published author. Inspired by my parents' resilience, I have become a leader in the Digital Tech space, empowering black women to enter the world of technology.

My father instilled in me the belief that to break free from societal norms, I needed to be exceptional in every endeavour. I excelled in my secondary school exams, undertook innovative projects during my university years, and surpassed expectations in male-dominated tech spaces. In 2013, I became intrigued by the future of work as identified by the World Economic Forum, particularly data science, machine learning, and artificial intelligence. I became a Lagos Nigeria Ambassador for Women in Data Science at Stanford University, championing the cause of black women in the data-driven age. I also established the ICT EduHub to support stay-at-home mothers and pursued advanced studies in England to further my knowledge of AI with Business Strategy.

However, my move to England revealed the biases and challenges I faced as a black woman. I experienced marginalization based on both my race and gender, leading to imposter syndrome.

I realized that individuals of African descent should bring their skills, services, and products to the world through social media, which negates my initial belief stemming from the cultural background of living for a cause and not applause, living to express not to impress, having my absence felt than making my presence noticed. I became intentional about amplifying my voice and making a difference.

In England, I joined Niyo Group where we empowered black women economically by upskilling them with digital technology skills and supporting their entry into tech roles or the launch of their businesses. Despite opposition along the way, such as being told I couldn't work somewhere because I was a woman and being denied a job because I was pregnant. These were tear-filled moments when I yearned for the ground to swallow me whole. I found a position in these oppositions, to demonstrate that the proof of the pudding is in the eating. These experiences fueled my passion to uplift and support black women.

Acknowledging the challenges faced by black women, I wrote an article titled "The Danger of a Single Story - Building AI Without Bias by Ensuring More Black Women Work in Data," which sparked widespread conversations. The article aimed to shed light on the need for increased representation of black women in the tech industry.

I am empowering my children to intentionally show up and speak up, fail first and fail fast, embrace resilience with grit and go for their passion, which takes them to heights their abilities cannot take them.

> " Show up &
> speak up,
> embrace
> resiliance
> with grit. "

Scan here to learn
more about
Chinazor

CLAUDETTE ATKINSON

SENIOR DIRECTOR IT DISTRIBUTION, PALO ALTO NETWORKS

"You can't say blackboard, and don't call her coloured!!!"

This is what my new team were told on the Friday before I started my job at an Insurance company way back in 1986! I didn't find out for months, and I finally plucked up the courage to ask a lady, who had largely ignored me for that time, what her problem was with me. Fearful of saying the wrong thing she had decided it was easier to say nothing. Ironically, we went on to become good friends.

I didn't choose Insurance, it was never a life goal, but after years of being told by my dad that I should be a doctor and studying A level Biology, Physics and Chemistry...I quickly realised that I didn't really like the sight of blood...that was never going to be an option for me.

There was no one to give me advice, I had 3 good grade A levels but, I thought, if I wasn't going to be a doctor, what else could I do? So, I left college and took the second job I was offered, earning exactly £4781 per year. I did this for a while, but watched with keen interest as my older brother came home describing his days in an IT company and how much more fun it seemed. Mine was so dull in comparison. Don't get me wrong I liked the people I worked with, but stories of people winning cars, bells being rung and cheers resounding round the office when a sale was made was a million miles from the library-like environment I worked in. I wanted that fun!

Fast forward to today and I run the Distribution channel, covering Europe, Middle East, Africa and Latin America for the largest Global Cybersecurity company. I love my job.

The journey to this point has not been easy, racism and misogyny were (and still are) common practice. My dad told me that I would have to work 3 times as hard as anyone else to succeed, so I did!

When I joined the IT industry I wondered how I would survive....I don't have a technical bone in my body. What I did have was a way with people and the ability to understand that it wasn't really about the technology, customers wanted outcomes. This was right up my street, I was curious and intelligent, so I found my niche. I like to have fun as well as getting the job done, and working with Distributors in IT gave me that. I have heard the sales bell ring many times through my career.

Years ago, I remember saying that I wanted to be the first black female director in UK Distribution...I did that, and more...my current job is Senior Director, Distribution at Palo Alto Networks.

Sadly, there are no others that I am aware of...so my mission is to support and mentor young black people in Tech, so there are others behind me...who, no doubt will go further than me!

"
Support
& mentor
young black
people in
tech.
"

Scan here to learn
more about
Claudette

DANIELA NYARKO

SALES LEAD - EMEA, CANVA

My family migrated from Ghana and I was born and raised in Germany. I was always inquisitive so my mom and grandma encouraged me to explore a variety of interests such as sports, music, and art. I took full advantage of this opportunity, participating in creative projects and excelling in sports and dance. My passion for dancing led me to join a community dance group that went on to win national and European championships, which was a remarkable experience and in some way my first tangible taste of success and failure.

My first few years of secondary school were challenging, and I struggled to adapt and find joy in my studies. However, I excelled when I moved schools and discovered a more supportive environment. Although it wasn't the start I had envisioned and it wasn't going according to plan, my mother gave me a piece of advice that has stuck with me ever since: "Daniela, your past does not define your future. Focus on the present and the impact you can make now for your tomorrow."

Although my mother wasn't the image of a traditional German role model, her immigrant background and unique cultural perspective gave her a captivating grace and excellence that set her apart. Despite facing numerous challenges, she owned and operated a small business that served as a testament to her unwavering commitment and determination. Her example has instilled in me an early appreciation for perseverance and the importance of continuing the journey, regardless of one's background or current situation. So, in 2010 after enrolling at multiple universities and starting different degrees in Germany and the Netherlands to find a suitable course, I moved to London. It was time for a change and a turning point in my life. I learned so much about myself and my capabilities.

For the very first time I was surrounded by so many inspiring black men and women, empowering me to aim higher. I landed my first graduate job in account management, but it was my job in Canary Wharf that exposed me to the power of technology and its impact on our lives.

I was fascinated by how organisations used technology to make business decisions, stay ahead of competitors, and respond to trends. I realised that tech is not only about fancy gadgets. It is about how technology can be used to solve real-world problems and make a positive impact on people's lives. The fact is that technology is transforming how we move, make decisions and engage. Drawing on a decade of experience in the tech sector, I've observed a notable gap in gender and cultural diversity, compelling me to become a dedicated advocate for inclusivity in the field.

One of my previous bosses helped me to unlock my leadership skills, allowed me to grow into various positions and later promoted me to the Head of alliances in EMEA. I believe that building strong teams and bridges to success requires a diverse range of perspectives, whether they're influenced by gender, culture, or individuality in general. When combined, these unique differences have the power to make a difference even beyond our professional lives. There is so much room for every single one of us to succeed and all we need to do is be courageous and tap into our potential.

The piece of advice I would give to my younger self is.. Be patient, be kind to yourself and stick to your core values. You will make mistakes, but if you learn from your failures you have the power to turn them into compelling narratives.

> # "
> Be patient,
> be kind to
> yourself, &
> stick to your
> core values.
> "

Scan here to
learn more about
Daniela

DARVA SATCHER

DIRECTOR OF ENGINEERING, GITLAB

The sun was shining, and the birds were chirping; however, I recall looking down at my sweaty palms and feeling the uneasiness of butterflies in my stomach. I looked up at the clear blue California sky and began daydreaming about what had led me to this moment...

In the 1980s, I was a thin, brown-skinned girl living in Oakland, CA. I enjoyed reading, playing video games, and solving puzzles. My mom would tell us to play in our backyard due to her safety concerns in our neighborhood. Our city had your typical urban city crime and underfunded schools. My world was small back then. I wanted to grow up, get a job, and earn enough money to pay my bills.

In 1991, I watched a film, "Boyz n the Hood." One of the main characters lived in a rough neighborhood. She escaped her environment by enrolling in an all-women's historically black college, Spelman College.

The seed had been planted.

In 1992, I walked onto Spelman's campus. Many inspiring African American women came to Spelman to share their wisdom and experiences. We heard from College Presidents, Scientists, and CEOs. As I listened to each woman's story, my world grew.

...Once I finished daydreaming, I headed to the career fair. My nerves were gone. With confidence, I walked into my first tech job interview. Four middle-aged men from a large American Company were seated at a long white table across from me.

During the hour-long interview, I explained my qualifications in great detail. I was pleased with how well I had done. However, I was shocked by what came next. One interviewer said, "You performed poorly during this interview and will never work for a large American company."

I exited the interview and ran into a nearby classroom. I had another interview scheduled within the hour. I wanted to burst into tears and run to my dorm. However, my past experiences taught me that you keep moving forward when you fall. Don't retreat. I reached into my bag, pulled out a copy of my resume, and began preparing for my next interview.

The following month, I received multiple job offers. I accepted an offer from IBM as a Computer Engineer. IBM, by the way, is a large American company. That day I learned that I tell my story: not a table of strangers.

That tiny seed planted years ago has since flourished and continues to grow. Today, I am a Director of Engineering for a global company. Now I am the face the young brown-skinned girl sees when she walks confidently into her first tech job interview.

Education is freedom.

Scan here to learn more about Darva

DONNA HUSSEY

DEVELOPER, THE NATIONAL ARCHIVES

I was born in North London and I was the middle child of parents of Caribbean heritage. My father was a carpenter and my mother would always tell me the story of how she came to England to become a Nurse. Instead my mother worked in local government in secretarial positions and front office for 40 years. My parents were very strict with my upbringing and academics, the route was given to me to do A-levels and go to university. I loved school and I was the first to go to university as my parents or grandparents never went on to higher education.

My life changed when I graduated from University where I met my children's father. Although I was planning to continue on to do a Masters on my year out I became pregnant. My parents were not supportive and I found myself homeless in my early twenties. I remained ambitious and continued to drive forward with lots of hard work throughout the years.

In my thirties I became a single parent. This did not hold me back as I supported my children and set up a successful business in schools with special needs, specifically offering Lego brick clubs in schools.

In my forties I began learning to code whilst home schooling. During the pandemic in 2020, it impacted the business. I could no longer go into schools, so I had to get everything online.

I'd always had an interest in tech which started with learning html and css online but nothing where I'd actually worked in a tech role. I decided to make a career change into tech. I started more self learning and completed a Code First Girls CFG Degree.

I applied for quite a few roles. As people know, when you're doing a career change, it's not easy because you're applying for roles you haven't had any on the job for experience in only transferable skills. So it's about companies giving you that first step, that first chance. I was fortunate to get a position with the Civil Service National Archives as a Developer in November 2022.

For me, this feels like just the start of my new adventures in tech even though I am in my 40s and a mother of three. I just feel really excited to have a dream job. I have volunteered to mentor others also I have been mentored. Over the years I have become an expert in school placements and have formed a group for parents BCIE Black Children in Indepenent Education. In the future I would like to help others with upward social mobility and parental support and education is at the heart of this.

My experience so far and will continue to be simply the three 'P's - Perseverance, Persistence and Patience.

I want to say to everyone...
If you want to do something just focus, plan and get it done!

Just focus, plan & get it done!

Scan here to learn more about Donna

DONNA OTCHERE

ECOSYSTEM PROGRAMME OFFICER, ROYAL ACADEMY OF ENGINEERING, COFOUNDER, SiSTEM

My journey started with a curiosity. I loved maths, it was the only subject I connected with straightaway besides from the arts. The arts were a place where I could express my creativity and maths just made sense. One day it hit me, what if I could be creative and academic at the same time? I did a quick google search and the first thing that appeared on my screen was engineering. I instantly fell in love. The job description was everything I desired. The next day I went to my all-girls secondary school, I told everyone I wanted to be an engineer. I thought this moment would be one of celebration, the whole class would stop and cheer as I walked to the front and take a bow. All I heard were crickets. There was so much confusion on my classmates faces. "You want to be a mechanic?". It was at this point, I realised that my dreams of becoming an engineer was not normal for a girl who was obsessed with fashion and YouTube makeup tutorials.

Despite the lack of understanding of engineering from the people around me, I continued to pursue the career. I had the support of my older sister and mum, they couldn't quite comprehend what the industry was, but they knew it made me happy. I had an uncle in Ghana who was an electrical engineer, I thought when he heard the news of me pursing engineering, he would welcome me with warm arms. He told me I need tough skin and I should stop wearing makeup. Even though I was quite young and impressionable, I still had a gut feeling that his opinion was wrong. I finished my GCSEs and left my school winning over the support of my peers and teachers, but the real battle began when I went to college and reality hit that the proportion of women studying subject like maths and physics was considerably low compared to men.

I didn't hide away. I was unapologetically myself. I began to struggle academically because there was a huge gap in the standard of education I received coming from a low social economic background. By the time I had finally got a good foundation of knowledge, it was too late however I was determined to be an engineer. I felt like it I did it I could make an impactful change to the industry; the dream wasn't just for me but for other girls too. I didn't have the entry grades, teachers told me to change careers, but I stuck to it and found a way into university to study mechanical engineering.

My story is not a smooth one, it is one full of failures, resistance, and rejection. If I didn't go through the hurdles, I would not be able to tell you today that despite your circumstances anything is possible if you put your mind to it. Dream bigger and unapologetically be you.

Dream bigger & unapologetically be you.

Scan here to learn
more about Donna

NORTH AMERICA

Scan here to learn more about North America's history

CANADA

Jean Augustine (1937-present)

A trailblazer and pioneer in the Canadian political landscape, as well as a dedicated and respected leader in the Black community. Augustine's journey from a young immigrant to the first Black woman elected to the House of Commons in Canada is a testament to her determination and hard work.

MASSACHUSSETTS

Sarah Parker Remond (1826-1894)

Sarah became an active member of the abolitionist movement and delivered powerful speeches on slavery, women's rights, and equality. She was a fierce advocate for the rights of African Americans and used her platform to raise awareness about the injustices and cruelty of slavery.

NEW YORK

Sojourner Truth (1797-1883)

An African-American abolitionist and women's rights activist who lived in the 19th century. Born into slavery in New York, she was freed in 1826 and became an itinerant preacher, travelling around the country to speak out against slavery and for women's rights.

MARYLAND

Harriet Tubman (1822-1913)

An African American abolitionist, humanitarian, and an armed scout and spy for the United States Army during the American Civil War. Born into slavery in Maryland, Tubman escaped in 1849 and subsequently made some 13 missions to rescue approximately 70 enslaved people. During the Civil War, she served as an armed scout and spy for the Union Army. In her later years, Tubman was an activist in the movement for women's suffrage.

SOUTH CAROLINA

Mary McLeod Bethune (1875-1955)

Born to former slaves, she grew up in poverty but was determined to get an education. After working as a teacher, she founded the National Council of Negro Women in 1935 and was a leader in the National Association for the Advancement of Colored People (NAACP). She was also a strong advocate for women's rights and was appointed as a special advisor on minority affairs by President Franklin D. Roosevelt.

DOROTHY AKOH-ARREY

DIRECTOR OF DATA AND TECHNOLOGY, ACRE

Born prematurely in Yaoundé, Cameroon, to a French Cameroonian father and an anglophone mother, my path serves as a testament to the transformative power of seizing opportunities and embracing one's purpose.

Today, I find myself leading an exceptional team of Data and Technology specialists building CRM systems that drive value for companies. My journey towards this remarkable position began unexpectedly, during my time in London as a student working part time in fundraising, chugging buckets on the streets. My curiosity piqued, leading me to inquire about the destination of the data we were collecting. It was then that I realized the striking similarity between the work I had previously undertaken as a researcher at the Department of Journalism and Mass Communication, where I used SPSS to code and analyse communication data. I took a leap of faith and applied for a data administration role with Liberty Human Rights. This marked the beginning of my path in the realm of data, a decision that would shape the course of my career from leading charities like British Heart Foundation, Versus Arthritis, Leonard Cheshire, and commercial brands like Nespresso and now Acre (a leading sustainability Agency with global coverage) and a Microsoft Dynamics Case study on building segmentation using CRM intelligence.

Raised in a family with roots across West and Central Africa, I witnessed hardship firsthand. Following my parents' divorce when I was three, my family grappled with poverty.

Yet, my mother's tenacity and commitment to education, despite the circumstances, deeply inspired me. Tragedy struck when my younger brother suffered severe head injuries in an accident, intensifying the struggles we faced. Nevertheless, I continued to persevere, balancing part-time work with studies, with paid internships at Cameroon's leading Oil Refinery SONARA and later secured an internship at Macmillan publishers. Offered the position of editor for Cameroon, trained in the UK. I made significant contributions, including introducing the first-ever HIV/AIDS readers to the Cameroon curriculum and in 2010 founded my own charity Teach Me To Fish to support underprivilege children fund their education.

Throughout my professional journey, I've consistently wrestled with feelings of self-deprecation and uncertainty, as my accent often required me to code switch to fit in. Microaggressions and exclusion further reinforced that. However, exceptional mentors have served as inspiration to actualise my full potential. I am grateful for their support. Despite my achievements, I still work on embracing my accomplishments fully. In today's technologically advanced world, I encourage individuals to be curious, leveraging the power of information and connectivity, all at our fingertips for continuous learning.

My goal is to inspire others, especially young women, to embrace their potential and create their own paths. My ultimate desire is to see my children positively impact the world. My message is to encourage authenticity, kindness, and impact across businesses I work with. It is my firm belief that in a world driven by technology, the ability to learn, research, and share can truly shape a brighter future.

Embrace your potential & create your own paths.

Scan here to learn more about Dorothy

ELOHO KEMI

MACHINE LEARNING SCIENTIST, SS&C TECHNOLOGIES

So much of your career path can be determined by two things: Having the courage to change and knowing when to persist in the face of adversity.

At 19, I was diagnosed with dyslexia; later than is typical but, given my reasonable grades at school, it's not hard to see why. When all the unconscious coping mechanisms I had developed fell apart during my first year at university, I failed my exams and was finally diagnosed. I reflected and decided to switch courses from Psychology to Electronic Engineering; it was far from easy, but I built on my strengths, learned to cope with the diagnosis and graduated with a 2.1.

Despite obtaining a solid degree, I struggled to land interviews for graduate engineering roles so stumbled into construction when my neighbour recommended me for an admin role at her company. After a few months, I realised I wanted to apply my efforts to becoming a Quantity Surveyor but, before I could get the chance to upskill, the company collapsed.

Determined to continue, I landed an admin role at another construction company and told my manager my goal was to become a QS. During a performance review she told me I couldn't become a QS because of how messy my desk was, but 18 months and a well-honed application later, I landed that role as a Jr QS.

Two years on, I moved into an QS role at another company, working under an apathetic manager that had little interest in helping me grow within the company. I had also been diagnosed with ADHD, received minimal support from my superiors and yearned for something more technical and innovating, so after a particularly disappointing day at work, I'd had enough. I handed in my resignation and began research into technical roles with better pay and job satisfaction.

I came across the field of data science and was also reading the book "AI Super-Powers". This pushed me to begin teaching myself Python via YouTube videos but knew I needed more structure and accountability. I decided a coding bootcamp was the answer. After dozens of hours coding, researching, and applying, I struck gold. I landed a full scholarship for underrepresented groups in tech and started an intensive 10 week bootcamp.

For 3 months after the bootcamp, I applied for jobs non-stop, facing disappointment at every turn. I'd been unemployed for about 7 months, had taken out credit card debt to support myself and was starting to feel the pressure. After everything I had been through, I knew I had to keep going. Finally, at the end of May 2022 I applied for a Machine Learning Scientist role, and after several interview stages, I was offered the role and now work in a field I love, surrounded by peers who support me.

Wherever you are in your career, remember the biggest risk you take is not betting on yourself. Put in the work and what is for you will come to you.

The biggest risk is not betting on yourself.

Scan here to learn more about Eloho

DR. ELSA ZEKENG

FOUNDER & CEO, SÖKERDATA

I grew up in Cameroon, West and Central Africa, often known as 'Africa in miniature' because of its geographical and cultural diversity. I was always aware of my family's privileges, and later in life, realised that I grew up in what I call 'a cocoon' – a 'knowing' that between my parents' financial and intellectual capabilities, their relentless spirit in ensuring we strived for excellence, and my faith in God, almost anything was achievable. My mum, a pharmacist, owns a thriving pharmacy in the capital of Cameroon, Yaoundé. My dad, a scientist, led the National AIDS program in Cameroon and joined the United Nations programme on HIV/AIDS (UNAIDS) 20+ years ago. I attended a highly esteemed all-girl boarding school in Cameroon, Our Lady of Lourdes College, Bamenda where I completed secondary school. By virtue of being better at the sciences than the arts, and as a by-product of my home influence, studying science at A Level and eventually at university was the only logical route.

I moved back to the UK (I was born in Leeds) at age 15, where I attended an all-girl boarding school in Reading, Queen Anne's School Caversham. Clearly my parents had a mission to ensure that I stayed in all-girl schools. At the time, my naive mind, thought it was a way to ensure I stayed away from boys. Well, I learned later on that all-girls school provide an insular effect supporting girls to stay in STEM longer (usually up to and above graduate level) . I guess it is no surprise then that I went on to complete a B.Sc. in Molecular Biology with a year in industry followed by a Ph.D. in Infectious Disease and Global Health at the University of Liverpool.

9 months into my Ph.D., I had the realisation that while I loved science, staying in academia was not my preferred career path. I set out to 'find' or I now realise 'create' a career for myself. This led to me co-founding an organisation, the Northwest Biotech Initiative (NBI) to support student scientists seeking careers outside academia. Although no longer under my management, NBI is now in its 10th year, hosted over 50 events and supported 100+ students into employment. Committing myself to my interests, in 2015, during the biggest Ebola outbreak in West Africa, I deployed to Guinea with the World health Organisation (WHO). I spent 6 weeks working 12-14 hour days, 7 days a week testing 200+ samples for malaria and the Ebola virus. Upon my return to the United Kingdom, I received 'The Ebola Medal for Service in West Africa' from Her Majesty Queen Elizabeth, II (RIP). This experience left an indelible mark on me and so I became an advocate. I was selected by the European Commission as a European Development Days 2016 young leader to represent Sustainable Development Goal 3: Universal Healthcare for All. I debated on high-level panel meetings along with Mark Dybul, former Executive Director of Global Fund, and several other high-level executives on the importance of health equity and equal Global North-Global South power dynamics.

I now sit at the intersection of science, entrepreneurship and policy; as I quickly realised, these sectors require collaboration for efficient impact. I am founder of SökerData Ltd, a startup increasing ethnic minority representation in clinical trials, and championing health equity. I sit on several advisory boards: University of Salford, Science and Industry Museum Manchester and SmartWorks Manchester which supports women into work. I'm frequently invited to speak publicly about women and girls in STEM, clinical trial participation and Africa- Europe Partnerships. Life is more fulfilling than I could have imagined, and the risks paid off.

You are so much more capable than you can imagine.

Scan here to learn
more about Elsa

EMILLIA-ROSETTE NLANDU

PHD CANDIDATE IN ARTIFICIAL INTELLIGENCE, KINGSTON UNIVERSITY

My journey began in 2009 when I relocated from the Democratic Republic of Congo to the United Kingdom as a refugee. After waiting for years to reunite with my father, I could finally come. Upon arriving at Heathrow Airport, my father was right outside waiting with a broad smile, and he warmly kissed my forehead the second he held me with tears falling from his years. We then made our way to Middlesbrough, a city in the Northeast that I would call home for the next seven years.

The language barrier was my biggest challenge. Coming from a French-speaking country in Central Africa, I needed help communicating properly to make friends, study or adapt to the new culture I had embarrassed. Therefore, I spent my first year in the United Kingdom learning English through the ESOL program at Middlesbrough College—an English program designed for Speakers of Other Languages. During that time, one of my teachers recommended that I consider taking extra lessons since I was the youngest in my class and considered attending university. So I took Mathematics classes, which helped me secure a place into a full-time BTEC in ICT program. - This is when I was first exposed to computers and technology.

Growing up, I didn't have a computer or access to one. Upon completing the Business and Technology Education (BTEC) program in Information Communication Technology, I was able to gain enough knowledge to have the confidence to want to pursue a career in technology and therefore enrolled on the Access to Higher Education program, which provided me with the necessary accreditations to gain entry into the university as all my certifications from my country were not internationally recognised.

My father was not supportive of my study choices at the time as he did not believe that I would not find any work. His exact words were, the field you have chosen is not designed for people like us. He wanted me to follow a career in the medical sector. I had already fallen in love with technology at this point, and I wanted to code more, and I couldn't help my curiosity.

So I applied for a BSc in Computer Science at a few universities despite my father's fears and discouragement.

Fast forward, I was admitted to Teesside University, where I studied Computing for three years. To support myself financially, I worked part-time on weekends and some evenings while attending lectures during the day. Following graduation, I relocated to London and have secured multiple tech jobs. I am pursuing a PhD in Artificial Intelligence at Kingston University. I will be the first person in my entire family to hold a doctorate title once I complete my degree.

Following my experience, I've been mentoring people in similar paths and launched Cheetah Code Academy, a platform where I provide free tech training/coaching to individuals from minority backgrounds in the UK and across Africa. In the past two years, I have successfully trained over 400 individuals, and I hope to establish a physical school in the Democratic Republic of the Congo (DRC) to bridge the educational gap.

Reflecting on the journey, I would tell my younger self not always to overthink things and take more risks. She should not let her insecurities stop her and she is more intelligent than she thinks. Things will always fall into place as long as she puts in the work.

"

Things will
fall into
place if you
put in the
work.

"

Scan here to learn
more about
Emillia-Rosette

GERTRUDE CHILUFYA WESTRIN

DEVELOPER ADVOCATE, QLIK

My name is Gertrude, I am the eldest child in a family of eight, born in the Northern part of Zambia, raised in the capital city Lusaka and currently based in Lund, Sweden.

When I was young, I was taught to work hard and get good grades in school as that would set me up for a successful life, so I did. Always top 5 in my classes, got into a top university in Zambia and shortly after got a prestigious scholarship to study in Sweden at a top university. At this point, I believed I had achieved the good life I had worked so hard for.

Moving to Sweden, I quickly realised that hard work and good grades alone can not guarantee a "successful life". I now understand that "success" itself, is relative. For so long I believed it meant getting a high-paying job straight out of university, buying a house soon after, perhaps making the list of Forbes 30 under 30, building an empire in my field and living happily ever after with a family.

All this changed as soon as I moved to Sweden. For the first time in 16 years of school, I cleared my exams on 3rd attempt. It was a painful experience, I had built my identity around being school smart, which for me equalled perfection and getting things right on my first attempt. I was crashed when I could not get a job 11 months after graduation. I was no longer top 5, my confidence and identity were shattered.

I could not fathom how I was living in Sweden a place I thought would be the epitome of my success yet felt so small and irrelevant. Eventually, I decided I had come too far to allow myself to be defeated. I painfully accepted that I needed to unlearn what I believed was true about me, life and success. I needed to embrace the power of constantly questioning, reinventing myself and knowing that failure is all part of the journey of living a fulfilled life.

By this time I had learnt that there are very few black women working in tech, and there was a shortage of developers. I saw this as an opportunity and decided to challenge myself to become a developer. I took a 16-week Bootcamp with Pink Programming where I learnt the basics of frontend development and that was my entry into working in tech.

I am currently a Developer Advocate, a role that basically bridges the gap between internal development teams and external developer communities. I am very proud to be in this position because my daily tasks also take advantage of my knowledge in marketing and communications skills.

If I could offer advice to my younger self in any way, it would be that big dreams are valid, success is mine to take but need to understand that it means not always getting it right the first time and that's ok.

Big dreams are valid, success is mine to take.

Scan here to
learn more about
Gertrude

HONEY-BELL OKE

TEST LEAD & WOMEN IN TECH LEAD, VERSION 1

Nigeria is where I was born and raised. As the family's eldest child, I have an obligation to lead by example for my siblings. Although my parents invested in us equally, society constantly reminded me—both consciously and unconsciously—of my status as a woman, with more importance given to a man.

Some people thought I was a quiet girl who didn't have a voice and only wanted to please; I was the complete opposite; I just didn't like being the centre of attention. I had an insatiable curiosity. I was aware that I had a distinct mindset and a strong will, or as my mother would describe it, a quiet stubbornness. It was years later that I managed to harness this as my superpower.

I would describe my family as middle-class. My parents instilled in us the importance of education, and right from a young age, our future was pathed. I was to grow up and be a medical doctor; my younger sister, a chartered accountant; my other sister, a lawyer and my brother would follow in my father's footsteps in Engineering. That's all we knew.

Despite not being the smartest, I knew one thing for sure: I didn't want society to decide my destiny simply because I am a woman. Although I had no idea how I would do it, I will always be appreciative that my parents shared this perspective.

Like most children on the planet, I wanted to be an astronaut, but as I grew older, I realised that my passion for geography alone wouldn't get me to space, so I did a "180", stole my sister's predicted future career, and studied accounting. Did I love accounting? Not really, but I didn't hate it either. I proceeded to complete an MBA in finance.

The UK presented opportunities, for which I am grateful, I am also aware of the difficulties of being an immigrant and a woman of colour from an early age. It was while working at the bank that I wandered into the field of IT, primarily software testing. The technology industry offered opportunities for career advancement, and I am thankful to family, friends, mentors, and colleagues for their encouragement.

I have advanced to become a leader in technology. I also founded the Women in Technology Network a few years ago for my current organisation, and the support from my employer still amazes me. We have flourished from a group of 20 women to a network of over 700 women. Our goal is to create awareness, empowerment, and inspire the future generation on gender balance and equity.

I serve as evidence that you don't have to be an expert in coding to flourish in Tech. If you have faith in your own potential, you will do great things.

I would advise my younger self to smile more, make errors and learn from them before moving on, and follow your instincts. Never allow the opinions of others to determine who you are.

> # "
> Never allow the opinions of others to determine who you are.
> **"**

Scan here to learn more about Honey-Bell

IFEOMA NOELIN OKOLIE

PRODUCT SAFETY MANAGER & EDI NETWORK DEVELOPMENT LEAD

At the age of about five, growing up in a Nigerian University town, Nsukka, I knew I wanted to become an engineer; A dream whose actualisation journey would have many interesting twists and turns.

During my school years in Nigeria, there was a prevalent gender-career bias at the time and it was not common for young women to study engineering. However, I was demonstrating strong aptitudes in STEM subjects, such as mathematics, physics, chemistry and even in subjects like biology. So, my parents convinced me that since I was equally good at biological sciences, I might consider a career in medicine, rather than engineering. As academics themselves, they were ambitious for me and wanted me to go to university, but they thought the medical profession might be more accepting of women.

I therefore ended up studying medicine at a University in Nigeria for three years, but I soon realised it was not for me – just as I had clarity of purpose in wanting to pursue a career in engineering, I also knew Medicine was a vocation I just didn't feel called to. And hence I wasn't exceling as I was used to. It is so important to be passionate about what you do, and for me, that's engineering. So, knowing It was better to be a happy engineer than a miserable doctor, I moved to the UK to study chemical engineering and the rest is history.

After I got my chemical engineering degree from Aston University – graduating top of my class with the best chemical engineer award – and a Masters in process business management from Warwick University, I took up an internship with Fish4Dogs, a pet food company. It was my first opportunity to prove myself. I started as a quality engineer, and this became a quality manager role. I was able to build a structured quality management system, which was ISO9001 certified within just 10 months of joining the business – my first job was quite daunting, but amazing!

Since then, I have been fortunate to build an amazing career in functional safety engineering, delivering state-of-the-art safety solutions across multiple industries and globally renowned companies like Rockwell Automation, GSK, Elekta and Thales. At Thales, I'm a Product Safety Manager, leading safety solutions on innovative Aerospace and Defence Projects, as well as the Chair of the Race Ethnicity and Cultural Heritage (REACH) Employee Network. This career has also been coloured by multiple company and professional body recognitions. I am now a Chartered Engineer (CEng) and a Professionally Registered Functional Safety Engineer (FSEng), which are not just great recognitions to have, but sets an example for others to follow.

However, my story would be incomplete if I do not mention my duality as both a scientist and an artist, in equal measure – my flare for one, enhances the other. I am a poet, a choral music leader and soprano cantor and an amateur abstract photographer. My duality and the lessons of my 'Triple-Minority' (Black, Female and Artistic) career in engineering are the reasons why I'm a passionate advocate for STEAM careers and for people achieving their dreams. If a Black girl at a school can see that someone who looks like her can succeed in engineering, that is so powerful, because I know – 'You can't be, what you can't see!'.

"You can't be, what you can't see!"

Scan here to learn
more about Ifeoma

JESSICA OKONKWO

OWNER, TECH PERSPECTIVES NEWLETTER

Navigating the Tech Landscape on My Own Terms

From the dynamic streets of Peckham, an area of London marked by social and economic challenges, I embarked on a resolute mission to transcend expectations and carve a unique path. Amid a landscape where opportunities often felt scarce, I realized I couldn't wait for a predefined route. Instead, armed with resourcefulness, unshakable self-assurance, and a refusal to be confined by circumstances, I navigated the obstacles that lay ahead.

Within the tech realm, I encountered the twin hurdles of being a woman in a male-dominated field and personal adversities. Balancing these challenges against a backdrop of a tumultuous household and financial instability, I tapped into an unwavering inner strength that fueled my journey.

Rather than adhering to conventional education, I embraced an apprenticeship as my gateway into the tech industry. Starting as a marketing apprentice, I stumbled upon the captivating intersection of creativity and technology within web development. This discovery ignited a relentless pursuit of knowledge, propelling me forward despite the persistent specter of imposter syndrome and the absence of relatable role models.

Throughout this journey, I encountered and conquered numerous obstacles, sought solace in the guidance of supportive mentors, and utilized every available opportunity to share my experiences on prominent platforms. My aspirations extended beyond personal triumphs; I was on a mission to enact lasting changes across the industry. Through dedicated initiatives and projects, I endeavored to dismantle barriers and foster a culture of inclusivity in tech.

My tenacity remained unswerving, allowing me to obliterate the constraints that my background might have imposed. From defying expectations in Peckham to thriving within the intricate world of technology, my journey stands as a testament to the power of perseverance and self-assuredness.

As I near the culmination of this chapter, an exhilarating sense of anticipation courses through me. This journey isn't confined to my personal narrative; it's a larger narrative of reshaping the tech industry through diversity and innovation. I'm unwaveringly committed to catalyzing change, inspiring others to pursue their dreams irrespective of their circumstances.

And so, the tale unfolds, an ongoing testament to resilience. As a representative of unyielding determination, I'm committed to a future where diversity takes center stage in tech, and audacious dreams become tangible realities.

Audacious dreams become tangiable realities.

Scan here to learn more about Jessica

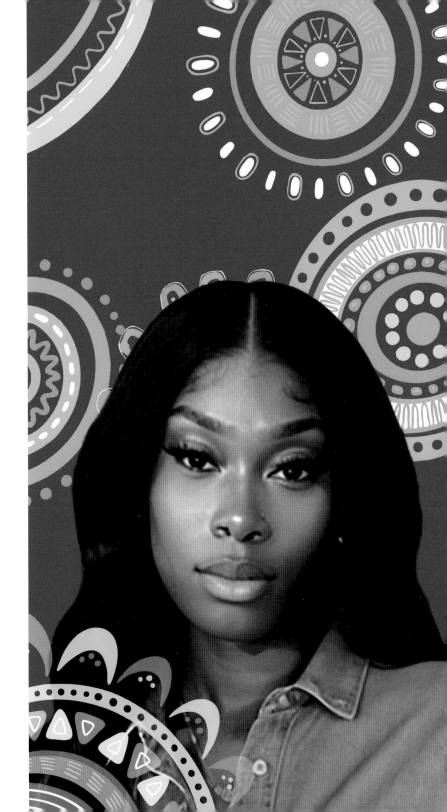

MAGDALENE AMEGASHITSI

SENIOR MANAGER, DIGITAL ADVISORY, AVANADE

Ghana, with its rich culture of family, home, and a wide variety of spicy food summarizes well the memories of my childhood. Born into a family of 7, we were not rich, but my parents made sure to provide us with enough and most importantly the peaceful and loving home needed for us to thrive. I still remember our black and white TV we watched at home until I turned 11 when my dad bought us a coloured TV which was revolutionary for me. As a child, I enjoyed learning which paved the way for me to become the first person in my family to attend University where I studied French and Spanish. I went on to study my Master of Science Degree in Economics at Strathclyde University in Glasgow, Scotland.

After my studies, I started working then got married, had kids, but then soon after, my life took a turn for the worse. Life really has a way of throwing lemons at you, and you can either allow yourself to be buried by them or make lemonade. What exactly am I trying to say? Well, overnight I became a single parent and had to continue my life journey single-handedly raising my toddler daughter and baby son alone. The sad truth is that financially it was impossible without changing career. I didn't want my kids to go hungry.

My career in Technology began after reading an article about data science and its high prospects. I went on to explore courses available and upskilled despite the difficulty of juggling with my full-time day job and parenting 2 little kids single-handedly, however, perseverance and tenacity took me through. I was so determined that before I had completed my course, I got my first Data Science role much to my relief.

Since then, I have enjoyed working for big companies delivering on major Transformation Projects and holding various Tech roles.

My career in Tech has been very fulfilling, and thanks to some amazing people I have met along the way, I have gone on to be shortlisted and winning some national awards. In 2019, I got selected as a role model, out of over 330 submissions, for the Tech Talent Charter's 'Doing It Anyway' Campaign launched in 2021. I have since been working with the Tech Talent Charter as an Ambassador on several initiatives to inspire Women into Tech and into Leadership.

In 2022, I won the TechWomen100 Award by WeAreTheCity UK. In addition, I was nominated and shortlisted in the Black Tech Achievements Award 'Employee of the Year' 2023.

Your legacy is every life you have touched; therefore, I setup the Women's Employee Network Group in 2019 to empower women in Avanade UK and inspire the younger generation through engagement with external charities supporting girls from less privileged backgrounds gain exposure to Tech.

Advice to my younger self will be, 'No matter how difficult things are, there is a silver-lining in the cloud'; also, 'Network extensively – it is truly your net worth'.

> **Network extensively - it is truly your net worth.**

Scan here to learn more about Magdalene

MAM JOOF

SOLUTIONS ARCHITECT, GIT LAB

I was born and raised in The Gambia, by my parents and aunt who was a nursery school teacher. As a child, I loved reading, taking part in drama and cooking.

Throughout my childhood, my parents wanted me to become a doctor and initially, I had convinced myself that this was the set path for me; but I knew deep down that it was not where my heart was. I had to figure out my own dream, so I made an agreement with my parents to allow me to spend one year reflecting and focusing on what I want to do next.

During this period of reflection, I got a job as a cashier in a bank and gained new skills and experiences. My interest in tech stemmed from working in the bank, when I happened to stumble across a server in the server room. This sparked curiosity in me and I was able to take this interest further by travelling to the UK to study a degree in Business Information Technology.

After graduating, I did not have a graduate job lined up and it made me reflect on what my close family and friends told me that "I had great interpersonal skills and can possibly be a great teacher." That was exactly the path I took. I made the life changing decision to go back to university and retrain to become a qualified Secondary School Computer Science teacher.

Upon qualifying, I taught Computer Science in Secondary Schools in London to inspire the next generation of technology stars. After four years of teaching, I discovered I was not enjoying the job anymore. So, I started looking for tech roles and became active on LinkedIn. I saw more inspirational black women in tech and was motivated that I could break into tech too. I changed my strategy this time and found mentors who gave me good advice and support. I applied and got accepted to a Software Development Community Bootcamp to strengthen my coding skills and get a job as a Software Developer. I completed the Bootcamp, but quickly realised that the Software Developer role wasn't for me, I quite frankly found it boring. With my mentors' support I was able to research different customer facing tech roles and realised that "Tech is more than just coding"!

Eventually, I got offered my first tech role as a Solutions Architect in GitLab. I have found ways to use my gift and make it stand out in my role whilst continuously learning other aspects of the role. Pursuing my career change aspirations unapologetically, while remaining wholeheartedly devoted to being a mother of three is possible, but requires an incredible amount of balance and mental focus. The struggle is real and the act of juggling multiple responsibilities at once is exceedingly real but if you're determined then you can do it.

If I could speak to my younger self, I would say embrace all that is you and celebrate your beautiful individuality.

Celebrate your beautiful individuality.

Scan here to learn more about Mam

MARIAM OPEMIPO OTAIKU

DATA ANALYST & PRODUCT LIAISON, FINANCIAL TIMES

I am a first generation immigrant, I was born in Nigeria and moved to London when I was 9. I am not here to tell a rags to riches story because ultimately, everything I have been through in life was meant to get me to exactly where I am today.

After graduating from University with a Law Degree, I was not sure I wanted to practice Law. I worked as a paralegal for 1 year and then went on to do a masters in Law because I thought I wanted to specialise in Human Rights Law. In the end, I ended up working in financial research at a tech startup. This was my first proper exposure to the world of tech and I loved it. I knew I wanted to upskill myself and become a "woman in tech" but with a non STEM / non technical background, I was often unsure where I could position myself. I tried a bit of everything - HTML, CSS and Javascript, looked into UX Research and even Cybersecurity. I was overwhelmed and was ready to give up. I felt I did not have a "career" and was just floating around in a "job". At the time I had no mentors so it was quite a lonely journey but my best friend at the time, who is now my husband, was always pushing me. He knew I would thrive within the tech space even though I did not believe it.

God has a way of directing the universe to lift me up when I need it the most. Late 2021, I decided to start self-learning data analytics. Before I knew it, in early 2022, I had a tutor who was teaching me SQL, Python and Tableau. I did not stop there, I enrolled myself in a bootcamp, joined several mentoring schemes (Black in Data and Black Valley) and got myself amazing data mentors. Mid 2022, I received an offer to join an insurtech company as a product data analyst. And to top it off, I am one of the recipients of the Office for students scholarship for Data Science which has enabled me to commence a part time masters in Data Science and Analytics at Brunel University. I look back at all these years and I am in awe of how much I have learned and how each season has led me to where I am today. I have a lot to share and no doubt plenty to learn.

If I could speak to my younger self, I would say...
It's never too late to start again. If there is a seat at the table, any table, you have every right to be on that table and you must not be put off even if it seems unattainable. You are not an impostor; you are deserving. Get ready to make strides within the tech space as a black muslim woman.

It's never too late to start again.

Scan here to
learn more about
Mariam

SOUTH AMERICA

Scan here to learn more about South America's history

VENEZUALA

Argelia Laya (1926-1997)

Argelia Laya was an Afro-Venezuelan educator and women's rights activist. She fought for women's suffrage and was one of the first to openly speak of a woman's right to have children outside of wedlock or obtain an abortion. She served as a guerrilla fighter for the communist party in Venezuela and she was one of the founders of the Movement to Socialism (MAS), pressing for anti-discrimination regulations to gain socio-economic parity for minorities, workers, and women.

PERU

Victoria Santa Cruz (1922-2014)

Victoria Santa Cruz was a Peruvian Afro-Peruvian singer, dancer, and social activist who is considered as one of the pioneers of the Afro-Peruvian music genre. From a young age, she was exposed to the rich culture and traditions of the Afro-Peruvian community, and it was here that she discovered her love for music and dance.

BRAZIL

Luiza Mahin (1800s)

A prominent figure in the history of Brazil and is remembered for her involvement in multiple slave revolts. Born in the 18th century, she was a slave who fought against the brutalities of slavery and the injustices inflicted upon her people. She was known for her bravery and leadership skills, which made her a respected figure among the enslaved communities.

URUGUAY

Virginia Brindis de Salas (1908-1958)

Virginia Brindis de Salas was the first published black woman writer in Uruguay. She was born on September 18, 1908 in the capital, Montevideo, to José Salas and Maria Blanca Rodriguez. Afro Latinos in Uruguay as elsewhere in Latin America are the descendants of enslaved people. In Uruguay, where 92 percent of citizens trace their ancestry to Europe, Afro and Native Uruguayans have had to fight for visibility, while whiteness has been emphasised in mainstream national life.

MARIAMA WURIE

PRODUCT ANALYST, GOOGLE

Black women are magic. Our very existence is an act of protest. Every achievement we make means the world to other Black girls and women.

Growing up, I didn't fully grasp the beauty of my skin color, my heritage, or my culture. The daughter of African immigrants, I had the usual parental guidance:

Be polite because it will be bad if you're ever anything less.

Work twice as hard because others will expect you to fail.

Education is your greatest asset and ticket to freedom.

Be a doctor because you should only strive for the best career (my Mom's opinion).

They wanted to protect me from any disadvantage of my skin color by being the hardest worker, the top of the class, the most well behaved. And to be honest, I was the best. Or I thought I was. I was #1 at my high school, the most polite child of my siblings, the shining star at after school activities. I got into and graduated from one of the best public universities in the US. I have been working for years at one of the biggest tech companies in the world. But becoming the star my parents had grinded into me from birth, didn't save me. No matter how much I achieved, I found myself burnt out, deep in mental illness, and still facing racism and microaggressions.

In my turmoil, it was a small comment that brought me back to life. After a panel, a Black woman messaged me, "Thank you for sharing your story. It means so much!" 12 seemingly tiny words turned me into a sobbing mess and seared into my brain – you are at your lowest and yet you mean something to your community. At that moment, I realized the one guiding principle my parents had missed, but saved me in the end:

Your Blackness is magic and anything you achieve (no matter how big or small) will change the world.

Surprisingly, I didn't realize how much working in tech had already helped me live by this rule. Because tech is fast-paced and opportunity focused, I was able to lean into my magic and share it with others. I led panels talking about my achievements. I had doors open for opportunities to learn more and teach more. I took my love for analytics and social justice and secured a role as an inclusion and equity analyst to make our products better. Tech was my game changer by helping me lean into my Black girl magic before even realizing it.

If I could speak to my younger self, I would say... Never forget your magic. I would remind her that her parents are only doing "their best" to protect her from a world designed for everyone else, and that "her best" (which doesn't have to be "the best") will make a world of difference to every single girl after her. You're magical honey. Keep going.

"

You're
magical
honey.
Keep going.

"

Scan here to learn
more about
Mariama

MARSHA CASTELLO

DATA ANALYST, UK CIVIL SERVICE & UN DELEGATE

I was born in the multicultural city of London, a vibrant cosmos enriched by its diversity of cultures. Born of the Windrush Generation, my Grandparents forged a life for us on these shores fortified from tremendous pride, courage, resilience, and pain. The inspirational story of this pioneering generation, and their vast contribution to Britain and a more egalitarian society through culture, talent, and labour, is poignantly outlined by works such as David Harewood's Richard Dimbleby lecture, available on BBC iPlayer, and Andrea Levy's novel, Small Island.

My mother, who arrived here from Jamaica, when she was 12 to join her parents, raised me with strong moral values, personal resilience, and an emphasis on education. All of which are a legacy of the Windrush generation and spirit. Education was drummed into me from an early age. With hopes that it would be an unshakable shield against adversity, a powerful sail on the voyage to self-discovery and a passport to opportunity, success, and social mobility. From modest beginnings, I was driven to achieve a master's in international business, have enjoyed opportunities working in trade policy, ministerial private office and currently data analytics.

Being the first in my friendship group to purchase the latest gadgets, I have always had a strong passion for technological innovations, tiny portals into future capabilities of humankind. Yet what powers it all? Data! The story behind everything. Through data, we learn of the motivational lessons of our predecessors, how our world works, and the many possibilities to shape our futures. I entered the data field after successfully securing a Performance Analytical role, later transitioning into Data Analysis with the UK Civil Service.

My interest in data has been further renewed by recently upskilling, certifying and gaining experience in programming languages Python, SQL and Java, and skill sets such as Advanced Data Analysis, Software Engineering, Cloud Computing, Project Management and AI & ML.

Along with great highs, there have been cavernous lows that I thought would swallow me: self-doubt, adversity, and the bereavements caused by the loss of close family members and friends to cancer. Through it all, great personal resilience, helped me to reframe those lows into turning points. Strengthening my resolve to honour those who have gone before me and adding weight, focus and urgency to my own personal dreams and aspirations. My future goals include using my competitive blend of skills and experience, to become a successful data engineer/ scientist and to inspire future generations, just as my parents and grandparents have inspired me. I actively share my knowledge through mentorship, my networks, STEM Ambassadorship and more recently as a UN Delegate to the Commission on the Status of Women, advocating for gender equality in education and technology. My advice to all would be to remain tenacious and unwavering in your quest for a better life and the best version of you. Know that you are deserving, that the world is awaiting your unique perspective and contribution. Set a blazing trail for others to follow!

The world
is awaiting
your unique
perspective &
contribution.

Scan here to learn
more about Marsha

MARY McCALLUM

FULL-STACK SOFTWARE ENGINEER, ORDNANCE SURVEY

I never considered myself to be a 'techie'. I just knew from an early age that I loved numbers, patterns and problem solving. This love has followed me in some way, shape or form my whole life.

I was born in London to Jamaican parents of the Windrush generation, who came to the UK in the 1960s. I was the third of four siblings, and the first girl of the family. Education was always a theme in our household: my mum taught me to read before I started school, as she wanted to give me a head start. Neither of my parents had any formal schooling, but they were determined that their children would. I'd always hear hallowed references to the professions of doctor, lawyer and teacher. But I never ever considered tech as a possibility.

Nevertheless, the signs were there. As a child, I figured out how to program our analogue TV by myself, with no manual. I spent my pocket money on puzzle books, seeking out as many of the logic problems as I could. My eldest brother, who had a keen interest in tech, told me: 'You could be a computer programmer', but all I could envision from that was sitting at a computer all day. It didn't pique my interest in the least.

Despite gaining my degree in Modern Foreign Languages with Education, the call to the tech world was never far away. When my eldest brother was doing a Master's degree in Cryptography, he requested help with the mathematical aspects of the course. I'd never heard of algorithms or modulus before, but I read the notes anyway and explained the concepts to him. He said that I should be the one studying on his course, that I was a natural, but I brushed it off light-heartedly.

After years in education, I started itching for a change. I realised that some traumatic experiences in my childhood and early career had left me feeling worthless, and had resulted in me playing small, especially in my work life. But I felt a deep desire to finally maximise my potential. When a friend asked me "Have you ever considered becoming a data scientist?", I had no idea what he was talking about. But he insisted that I'd be good at it. After some research, I felt Data Science wasn't for me, but it led me to discover Software Development. I was hooked.

I eventually signed up to a full-stack coding bootcamp, which helped me secure my first role in the tech field. I've now been in the tech space for over two years, getting paid to do what I love. Languages, patterns and problem solving have finally come full circle in my life.

If I could speak to my younger self, I would say...
Don't listen to the limiting voices. Your inner voice will always guide you to the right paths, places and people. If something ignites and inspires you, pursue it with all your heart.

"

Your inner voice will always guide you to the right paths.

"

Scan here to learn more about Mary

MIMI AJAYI

TECHNOLOGY DELIVERY LEAD, ACCENTURE

It is a privilege to share my story as a Black African woman now working in Accenture Technology. I hope that the highs and lows of my tech career journey will inspire others into tech.

My parents married in the UK as students and started a family before returning to Nigeria. My middle-class Nigerian family life included summers in England. I was born and raised in Lagos, highly progressive about women's education, career choices and financial independence. My family had a fairly British outlook relative to most. My earliest cultural diversity experience was foreign teachers, usually married to Nigerian men and their children in the same school.

I grew up as speaking English with my parents, and being a native speaker helped my tech career. My parents encouraged reading widely from their book collection. By about age 11, I'd read Chinua Achebe, Flora Nwapa, abridged works of Shakespeare and Oscar Wilde, Enid Blyton, while also learning to research meanings with dictionaries and the Encyclopaedia Britannica set. Fortunately, I was also picking up fluent Yoruba from my Granny who only knew a few English words. She left us a priceless gift of understanding rich Yoruba proverbs and tongue-twisters.

My siblings and I being two-culture kids, have an ease with both travelling to and living in various countries. My secondary school was full of girls from every corner of Nigeria, giving me exposure to another layer of our country's rich cultural diversity. Working in tech was not on my figurative radar by then. My impression of tech meant programming and Engineers or CS grads, meaning strong grades in maths and physics. That was not me, plus coding sounded boring anyway.

I graduated with a Psychology BSc. after re-sitting my O Levels. My learning style is not typical, in 2022 I finally discovered that I am neurodivergent. Among Nigerians from similar backgrounds, the typical rite of passage is to study, live and work a few years overseas, like our returnee parents. After a couple of clerical jobs, I relocated to London with big dreams to study for banking certification then return to Nigeria and join the banking boom. Instead, I worked in the City of London and Canary Wharf until the 2008 crash, having changed to advanced risk management certification.

Fast forward to 2017, and reconnecting with a childhood friend who'd changed to technology career from optometry. I'm thankful that she saw my risk management skills as highly transferable and kept encouraging me to consider a tech career as I was job hunting. In my now six-year tech career, I've worked in startups, mobile app delivery, a luxury retail and other large enterprise platforms. Accenture encourages certification, so I've gained AWS Certified Cloud Practitioner and SAFe. I've also prioritised my side project working on an EdTech platform.

To my younger self, I would say that you are smart, gorgeously melanin, creative and kind. Stop trying to fit in. Your empathy gives you discernment that will become your tech superpower in understanding customer needs. One day, you'll discover that your creative mind is fuelled by neurodivergence, then it will make sense why you notice details that others miss. Keep a calm mind because it makes your problem-solving mindset shine. Build your dream.

> " You are smart, gorgeously melanin, creative & kind. "

Scan here to learn more about Mimi

MONICA MEADE

HEAD OF TECHNOLOGY AUDIT, MASTERCARD

I was lucky to grow up on the Caribbean Island of Monserrat. I would get up early each morning to tend to my Uncle Robert's goats and other animals. And in the summer, there was the beautiful sea which was my playground...

Idyllic as this sounds, I knew that there were few opportunities for me in Monserrat. When I was fifteen, I went to stay with my granny in the UK. Over the next four months, we applied to three local schools, but all rejected me. I never found out why.

When I returned to Monserrat, I was disappointed but also very behind having lost four months of the final year of my exams. I was determined to catch-up, but my school refused to let me take all my subjects. My Mom wouldn't accept this and so she sent me to night school to study extra subjects alongside adult classmates.

One day as my friends and I walked home, we heard a loud explosion. We smelled sulphur gas and saw a large ash cloud looming above us. Terrified, we ran home along the coast path.

The eruption of the Soufrière Hills volcano came without warning. My dad led our family north to safety, but the volcano disrupted our lives, and my studies, for months. Our lessons took place in makeshift classrooms in strangers' houses. Whenever the electricity failed, as it often did, we had to work by candlelight.

But the studying paid off. When he heard that I got straight 'A's, my Uncle John, called. He asked me if I wanted to live with him and my aunt in the UK so that I could study for 'A' levels at Farnham.

I said, 'Yes,' before he even finished speaking, and before asking Mum and Dad.

I missed my family of course, and I worried about them because the volcano was still rumbling. And at Farnham College I faced some prejudice. But I'd been given an opportunity, and I wasn't going to waste it.

With University just a year away, I knew that I wanted to be financially independent, but I still didn't know what career to pursue. Then, flicking through the jobs in the Sunday Times, I noticed the salary for an 'Enterprise Risk Consultant'. And just like that, my decision was made.

The Times ad had specified that candidates needed a degree in 'Computer Science' and so I started studying for a two year Computer Science 'A' level in one year.

Later, when I told my college tutor that I was applying to King's College, she told me I wouldn't get in. But she was wrong. Since graduating I have enjoyed success with Deloitte, several prominent financial services companies and now Mastercard.

And so the advice I always give to young, ambitious black women is simply this: believe in yourself.

Believe in
yourself.

Scan here to learn
more about Monica

NATALIE SCARLETT

MANAGING DIRECTOR, TECH ROOTS

Tech is ... Hsgdfdydhuiut7tg75745dgffgxgfxnxgfxx bvx.

This is basically what I heard every time someone from a tech background spoke about tech. It always seemed like an exclusive club reserved for a particular type of computer whiz. If you feel anything like I did, applying for a tech role would have been something you could never see yourself doing, but oh how times have changed. I am here to tell you that YOU belong in tech because tech is no longer an industry; it is THE industry. I want to share how my "weakness" was nurtured by agile frameworks. But first I need to go back, way back.

It was my first day of school, my blazer was twice the size of me and still is to be honest because I haven't grown. Anyway, my Jamaican Dad handed me a bus pass, it cost him £65.45. He said four words that would follow me for the rest of my life.
Natalie, "Do not lose it!"
"No Dad, I won't"

I lost it within 24 hours. Similarly my Mom sent me to the cash point and said "Withdraw 30 pounds".
Here were those words again "Do not lose it!"
I went to the cash point, came back and my mom asks, "Where's the money?"
"Oh, yea" I replied.

I'd left it peaking out of the cash machine. I was forgetful, clumsy and unreliable. My year 6 school teacher, Mr fowkes told my two Caribbean immigrant parents that I would never go to University. What he saw as poor behaviour was ADHD playing out in real life, except there was no grace afforded to little Black girls like me. According to an NHS study, Black women are the group most likely to screen positive for ADHD.

However they will likely go undiagnosed as their symptoms are deemed to be disruptive and aggressive. What I realised as a child is that even though I had many flaws, I always had ideas and lots of them. Whilst ADHD can be debilitating with the burden of constant mind chatter and rumination, within that mind chatter lies the solution to some of the worlds greatest problems and that is why neurodivergent people like me excel in creative spaces.

I never thought of myself as a designer until I entered the tech space. I became a Delivery Manager, delivering services and product for companies. Delivery Managers are the glue that brings tech teams together. All you need is a vision, creativity and to be able to foster an environment of innovation. What I realised was whist I was in a wonderfully progressive space, there were very few Black faces and most people in my team did not have degrees, even the engineers. This is an open door for those who couldn't afford to go to University, the problem is that many people do not know these roles exist.

Delivery and using agile was a pivitol point in my career because it catapulted my skills and enabled my soft & creative talents to thrive in the hands of agile. These methodologies created an adhd friendly zone with the removal of jargon, introducing collaboration, getting rid of lengthy meetings and long documentation.

Having seen how frontline facing the Black Uk demographic is, I set out to transition as many people into tech as possible, by designing an exhibition that would have a taster of 'no coding' tech roles whilst making those taster sessions culturally relatable. Tech Rootz is unique, innovative and impactful.

> "Believe in the value you add, nobody can ever take it away from you.

Scan here to learn more about Natalie

NNENNA I. STEVENSON

PRODUCT MANAGER, SAPPHIRE STEVENSON LTD

Being born and raised in Nigeria to a Chartered Accountant and a Medical Doctor meant two things (other than the strict upbringing):

(1) that I had to enjoy studying and be nothing short of excellent

(2) I had only 3 occupations to choose from: "Doctor, Lawyer or Engineer". Unfortunately, I did not enjoy studying (so the first two occupations were off my list), and I thought I hated mathematics (so no hope of becoming an Engineer).

But I enjoyed writing, listening to others, understanding perspectives, negotiating my way out of trouble, and communicating for those who couldn't explain their problems (*inserts memory of me explaining to my mum that my wailing sister didn't mean to break the glass cup*).

At age 12, I never knew these were all the qualities I needed to achieve my fulfilling career- if I had known, I would have stopped being angry at my grades and would have been less resentful at being born with Sickle Cell Disease.

At 16, since I enjoyed playing computer games, my parents reluctantly allowed me to study Computer Science at University- they said I had suffered enough with the health condition and didn't want it worsened by forcing me to study something else.

That was the best decision they made! My first degree led me into a new world; I saw myself coding and creating documentation to explain the project software I had built (in Visual Basic, hehe!).

During Uni, I noticed my friends would ask me to teach them the maths courses— like, me, teach maths? Unbelievable! Little by little, I discovered more of my strengths and gained confidence- I mean, people called me "smart".

Later, I got into Gaming (Virtual Reality) and could not believe how exciting it was. IT, being a male-dominated field, made women think it was scary. But getting into it showed me how easy and learnable STEM (Science, Technology, Engineering and Mathematics) can be.

The best part of being a Computing Graduate is that when I decided that coding was no longer my path, I still found a field in IT that suited me- Business Analysis and Product Management. Now I could bring my personality & emotional intelligence into my work, enjoy helping users and businesses achieve goals, earn great compensation, experience career progression, and manage my health better by working from home for progressive companies that put their Staff's well-being first-- it's unreal!

And, if in the future I decide on another path like Teaching or Writing, I will be able to achieve this because Computing is Pervasive and flexible.

This voice in the shadow is whispering to you that STEM may look scary and hard, but I assure you, if you can hack the Multiplication Table, you can hack STEM, and anything you want to become in life can be achieved through it. Sometimes you need a leap of faith to see that nothing can hold you back, not even a health condition or non-excellent grades.

66

Sometimes
you need a
leap of faith
to see that
nothing can
hold you
back.

99

Scan here to
learn more about
Nnenna

NONDUMISO JIRI

PROJECT MANAGER/ DELIVERY LEAD, ACCENTURE

I was born in a small village in rural South Africa, where I spent my early childhood years. My family then moved to a small town where I spent the rest of my formative years.

After matriculating, I attended Rhodes University. My intention was to study a degree in accounting, but one day during a Computer Science 101 practical, my lecturer asked me if I would be interested in doing Computer Science 102 because she felt I had a knack for it. I didn't really take her seriously, but I went ahead and registered for it, and soon found accounting boring. I changed my major and graduated with an Information Systems degree.

When I was in the 10th grade, my parents made the decision that my mom would move to the UK for work purposes as a registered nurse and this helped ease the burden of university fees on the family. My parents wanted us to graduate without having the burden of paying off student loans. This is a sacrifice I will forever be grateful for.

My first job was not in the technology space, but it instilled hard work, discipline and dealing multiple clients which I use every day in my present role as a Technology Consultant. My career in technology kicked off when I was chosen as a part of ten graduates to join a South African mobile network operator's graduate programme. After 12 months' rotation, I was incubated as a Value -Added Services Specialist in the networks team. I then moved on to a company providing software and services for the automotive and insurance claims processing industry, working as a Technical Business Analyst within Product Development.

I decided I missed the telecommunications space and moved on Vodacom, where I worked as a Technical BA until I left South Africa in 2017.

While I was at Vodacom, I decided it would be great to work for a consultancy as I felt multi-industry technical experience would be beneficial to my career. One day I came across a Business Analyst role advert by a global consulting company and I applied as I felt the global experience would do my career world of good. I went through a tough three round virtual interview process over a period of three months. I was successful and got hired by Accenture UK.

I have been in the UK for six years and have worked with aerospace and defence clients as well as telecommunications clients in Business Analyst, Project Management and Delivery Lead roles.

My aspiration is to keep learning, growing, and advancing my career, which will put me in a position one day to share that knowledge with others, especially young girls who come from where I am from, so that they can also step up and take up space on the world stage. I want to show them that all their dreams are valid and possible, and they should go forth boldly and achieve them no matter where they come from in the world.

Go forth boldy & achieve your dreams.

Scan here to learn more about Nondumiso

OLUWATOSIN SONUBI

DATA ENGINEER, FINANCIAL CONDUCT AUTHORITY

As far back as I can remember, I have always had a head full of ideas and questions. I am a daydreamer.

Despite appearing to do well in school, I often struggled silently. I experienced a lot of anxiety and couldn't read until the age of 12. Though, I hid all of this because I feared standing out more than I already did, as one of few black young people in the English countryside.

So I focused my attention elsewhere. I spent the vast majority of my formative years fascinated, more accurately obsessed, with food. Consuming it, making it, learning about the science behind it: but mostly the creating recipes.

The fact that I could get some of my whimsical ideas out of my head and into reality amazed me, and still does. But during my youth, I was fortunate enough to meet some amazing engineers, who made the connection between my experimental recipe process and engineering.

Once I decided I wanted to become an engineer, I didn't let anything stop me. I faced obstacles in so many forms, but I saw these all as opportunities to take a new perspective.

When it came time to apply for university, I was concerned about the financial burden it would place on myself and my family, so I sought out scholarships, grants, and programs which not only aided me financially but allowed me to engage with people far beyond my personal network.

Furthermore, when I arrived at university and felt underrepresented, I took action and collaborated with my peers to create and run the Warwick Women in Engineering and Science Society (WWES), which became a safe haven for me and people like me.

It was the sisterhood and relationships I had established at WWES which pushed me and supported me, even post-university. Without their support, I would have never had the confidence to transition from conventional engineering to software/data, and teach myself to code.

As I entered the world of work, this empowered me and has driven me to achieve so many of my goals within such a short time span. When I reflect on all I have been able to achieve in my work in data, I am overjoyed.

I have taken so many opportunities that have come my way, which has allowed me to speak at conferences, support others in their pursuit of STEM, and technically contribute to large projects. This is only the beginning for me. I still have my head full of ideas and questions, and I'm excited to bring them into reality and contribute to something bigger than me.

" I'm excited to contribute to something bigger than me.

Scan here to learn more about Oluwatosin

ONYINYE UDOKPORO

FOUNDER, ENRICH LEARNING

My journey in tech began from a place of pain. I was being bullied whilst I was in primary school. I was different. Unknown to my teacher and I, I was (and still am) dyslexic. I struggled with reading, writing and spelling. My teachers would have to repeat themselves often because I needed to hear instructions a few times to comprehend what was being asked of me. I was slightly awkward with other students which only led to more bullying. I was known as the 'try hard'. I achieved great grades academically despite my troubles with reading, writing and spelling. This was due to my relentless work ethic. Throughout my life the narrative that I was told was that I needed to try harder than my peers: firstly, because I am a black woman, secondly, because I am neurodivergent.

I found comfort in my information technology classes. They were my escape. My I.T teacher was one of the kindest people I have ever met. She saw my enthusiasm and took me under her wing. At 8 years old my skill set with Excel was somewhat advanced - in actual fact, many a time, unknown to my parents, I used Excel to do my maths homework (sorry mum and dad)!

By the age of 9 I had learnt how to create my own websites. My teacher taught me basic html code. I began to look forward to my break times because it became an opportunity to build my computing skills. The computer room was my refuge...my safe haven. The 'cool' kids who didn't want to play with me became my best friends as I was able to assist them with their I.T work in class.

Fast forward 10 years later, using the I.T skills I developed as a result of being pained by bullying, I built the website of my online tuition business.

This tuition business has gone on to serve people globally, giving access to opportunities using education as a tool. Presently, I am now using my I.T skills to collaborate with developers and design neuro-inclusive digital learning tools as well as safely integrate the use of artificial intelligence to help users learn more about neurodiversity.

My journey in tech began from a place of pain but with resilience I transformed that pain into power and used my skill set to be of service to others. My point of difference was, and still is, at the centre of my destiny.

For those of you reading this, I want you to know that your difference is at the centre of your destiny too. Don't run away from it, run towards it and use it to empower, uplift and inspire others.

Your pain can and will, become your most pertinent power.

> " Your pain can and will, become your most pertinent power. "

Scan here to learn more about Onyinye

THE MIDDLE EAST

Scan here to learn more about the Middle East's history

SAUDI ARABIA

Tarouf Abdulkhair Adam Muhammad al-Talal Hawsawi (1947-2007)

Etab was a Saudi Arabian singer who was active between the 1960s and the 1990s. She was born in Saudi Arabia of Hausa descent, but migrated to Egypt shortly after her second marriage to an Egyptian man in 1978. Many Arab music experts agree that she was expelled from Saudi Arabia on the instructions of then-King Khalid because her musical performances were deemed risqué in Saudi Arabia at the time. She became an Egyptian citizen in 1983.

Etab, regarded one of the first female Saudi vocalists, began performing at weddings in the 1960s with Sarah Osman and oud player Hayat Saleh. She released over 15 albums and featured in three films. She was diagnosed with cancer in 1997 and died on August 19, 2007, in Cairo.

LEBANON

Mary Lee Mills (1912-2010)

Mary Lee Mills was born in 1912 and passed away in 2010, leaving behind a legacy of dedication and passion for nursing. She was a well-known figure in the nursing community, having established the first nursing school in Lebanon in the mid-20th century. She devoted her life to providing quality education to aspiring nurses, helping to improve healthcare in the region.

The nursing school established by Mary Lee Mills was a landmark in Lebanon, providing comprehensive training to those interested in pursuing a career in nursing. The school aimed to produce well-trained, compassionate and competent nurses, who would be able to make a positive impact in the healthcare sector. The curriculum was designed to cover all aspects of nursing, including anatomy, pharmacology, clinical practices and patient care.

The school played a vital role in the development of the healthcare system in Lebanon, providing highly skilled and trained nurses who helped to improve patient care and outcomes. Mary Lee Mills' unwavering commitment to nursing education and her tireless efforts to promote the nursing profession inspired many students to pursue a career in nursing, making a lasting impact on the nursing community in Lebanon.

PENNY EZECHIE

GLOBAL HEAD OF TRANSITION & CHANGE MANAGEMENT & DIRECTOR, DEUTSCHE BANK

I was born in Battersea, South London, 1st generation British to Nigerian parents. I was a quiet child in a large noisy and very intelligent family. The often spoken family ethos was "if you work hard you will surely succeed" and I did just that to everything I turned my attention to.

My father was one of the first black Barristers in the UK and although I am incredibly proud of his achievements, I knew I did not want to follow in his footsteps. Science was my first love.

I traveled to school in Wimbledon by train, I remember seeing hundreds of people going in the other direction. Where were all these white people going? I figured that was where the money had to be so I decided I would work there. "There" ended up being the City.

After Uni, I landed my first job working for a Stock Brokers. I worked hard and progressed up the ranks quickly, becoming manager of the IT department within just 3 years. With frequent and increasing acquisitions and mergers my role and experience grew, that was all good whist my company was doing the buying but when we were acquired everything changed. I hit my first brick wall, I would now be reporting to the new CTO as would a male peer "John", who was Head of Facilities, we had a joint meeting with the new manager.

In the meeting the CTO asks questions about IT to John. John says, "Penny is Head of IT", I take the question and give the answer. The CTO barely acknowledges me. He asks another tech question to John, I jump in and respond again and this is how the entire meeting goes. He barely even looks at me.

When the meeting ends, I go to the bathroom and cry.

Where do I go from here? I have a job I love, have been recognised and rewarded for but my new boss cannot even look me in the face. I was alone trying to navigate this and from my perspective ahead was a future of being ignored, bypassed and sidelined.

I have no sponsor no mentor no network that I can share this with. The only other black people in this organisation are a secretary, a receptionist and the security guards. Who is going to understand? I don't want to go to HR and be asked how do I know it is racism or chauvinism. Long story short I quit.

In time, I picked myself up, found another job, and grew my network. I actively elicited sponsors and cultivated my boardroom of mentors and I never looked back. I'm pleased to say in my career I have had more highs than lows. If I had my time again there is much I would do differently which is why I am such a vocal and visible advocate for Black people and women in Technology today, I share my experience and give advice to help others avoid the same pitfalls.

If I could tell my younger self one thing it would be you absolutely do belong and you are enough, now go slay!

> " You absolutely do belong & you are enough, now go slay! "

Scan here to learn more about Penny

RAMAT TEJANI

STRATEGIC PARTNERSHIPS LEAD, GOOGLE

Whatever I decide to do in the future, I want to be a successful and happy woman, who cares for others and is always willing to give people my help and advice.

Those are the last words of the autobiographical essay I wrote as part of an English assignment when I was 14. Even then, I knew one of my many callings in life is to help others.

One of the ways I currently do this is in my role as a Strategic Partnerships Lead for EMEA in the Diversity Recruiting team at Google. In this capacity I work to build and nurture strategic partners that can help diversify the talent pipeline with a focus on the Black community. Technology has the power to change the world and yet the industry rarely represents the diversity of the audience it serves around the world. I have intentionally chosen to work in global organisations over the years as I try to impact as many people as possible.

Prior to this role, I was responsible for scaling Amazon's biggest education program, AWS GetIT. I grew it across EMEA in the UK, Ireland, Germany, Spain, Italy and Israel and launched the pilot in Singapore, as the Education Programme Lead. The programme had two main objectives. Firstly to take women from across the company through an executive speaker training programme empowering them to take up space and use their voices into instruments of transformation. And secondly, for the women to then become mentors to students in schools taking part in our regional competitions to encourage young, in particular girls to consider a career in technology.

My journey to working at global tech giants like Google and Amazon hasn't been without its challenges, and yet I wouldn't change a thing. Born to Ghanaian parents, I am the eldest of three daughters. I was born and raised in the amazing cultural melting pot of East London where there were always at least two other languages being spoken around you. So you can imagine my shock when I entered the working world after university to find a world in which very few people looked like me. I had to anchor myself on a phrase I often share when delivering keynote speeches or workshops, "No one is coming to save you." Afterall, at the end of the day despite all the help people may give you, YOU ultimately need to do the work. Creating a personal manifesto helped to ground me whenever I felt myself veering off my personal path. My TEDx talk, 'The Transformative Power of a Personal Manifesto' was and still is a reminder to myself and whoever needs to hear it; that your journey cannot be navigated by anyone else's compass - so embrace it.

The echo of my teenage voice still whispers truths today. As you climb life's staircase, remember to cast the occasional glance backward. Hopefully it'll serve a reminder to find ways to help those coming up behind you.

To my younger self I would say...
Remember your brilliance even when others don't. Picture yourself as a phoenix, especially when life feels hard. You will emerge from the ashes of life tribulations. You will spread your wings. And you will rise again. You've got this.

"
Remember your brilliance even when others don't.
"

Scan here to learn more about Ramat

DR. RASHADA HARRY

ENTERPRISE TECHNOLOGIST & FOUNDER
AMAZON WEB SERVICES & YOUR FUTURE, YOUR AMBITION

I have always given my best towards every opportunity. Like most students, some aspects of academia were more challenging than others.

In my final years of my undergraduate degree, I regularly attended the 24-hour library to ensure that I stayed on top of my grades, and it paid off. I was offered a 'conditional' place at a prestigious London University to study a master's degree in law. I was over the moon! I just had to pass my exams the following year.

It wasn't until one of my tutors looked over my exam papers and suggested I should be tested for dyslexia, that I considered for the first time that this may explain why my grades did not always reflect my study efforts and commitment.

I was subsequently diagnosed with dyslexia in my final semester at university. It was a blow that I didn't quite understand or know how to respond to. Over time, with the support from family and tutors, I accepted and embraced my diagnosis.

As I awaited my final exam results, I was naturally nervous; a lot was resting on the opportunity to attend a world-renowned university. The results came in, and sadly, I was just two marks away from the grade that I needed. I was devastated.

The university told me my place would be offered to someone else on their very long waiting list. I desperately wanted to keep my place, the place that I worked so incredibly hard for. I was told all appeals would take place three weeks after the autumn term, therefore commencing in September.

It was a long and tearful summer, not what I had anticipated. I didn't have a back-up plan.

I anxiously presented my appeal to the panel, explaining that I was not aware of the limitations my learning disability had caused, but with support, I was confident I could pass. The panel reviewed my application, and whilst they agreed with support, I would be a suitable candidate they didn't feel I could catch up from three weeks of missed lectures and seminars. I reached into my backpack and presented a folder that contained my full set of notes from each class. Although I wasn't able to enrol, I attended every lecture and seminar, sitting quietly at the back of the room.

The panel were astonished and impressed by my enthusiasm, dedication, and commitment. My appeal was approved on the spot, and I continued on the course.

After a lot of hard work and a great support system, I am pleased to say that I now hold a LLM Master of Laws degree from the London School of Economics.

My advice to any young girl is to keep going. Sometimes, unexpected challenges and bumps in the road will arise, causing delays and detours. It may feel unfair unexpected, but please keep going. With every (perceived) failure, closed door, or re-direction in your journey, there is a lesson to be learned to make reaching your destination that bit more rewarding.

My lesson was understanding the importance of resilience, belief in my own ability, and determination. I didn't give up. I was prepared to keep knocking and pushing the door open.

"Lessons learned make the final destination more rewarding."

Scan here to learn more about Rashada

ROSA EMILIA REMEDOR AVENDAÑO

GLOBAL TRAINING & QUALITY MANAGER, ACCENTURE

My name is Rosa Remedor, and I'm excited to share my story as a Mixed Race Black woman in Accenture, with the hope that I can provide insight and representation for those who need to see it. I was born in Venezuela to a Venezuelan mother and a Haitian father, which provided me with a unique upbringing immersed in rich cultural diversity from both my parents' backgrounds. However, due to Venezuela's current socio-economic situation, most of my family and friends now live abroad, including my brother, Joseph Remedor who resides in Peru.

Growing up in Venezuela was an enriching experience, but as a person of mixed race, I often found myself being the darkest person in the room, whether at school, college, or work. The lack of representation was evident not only in my immediate surroundings but also in the media. It became the norm to believe that success for someone like me could only be achieved through exceptional accomplishments, and high-ranking roles seemed unlikely for people of colour. After completing high school, I discovered my passion for marketing and pursued a degree. This educational foundation provided me with the opportunity to work in banking for Santander in Venezuela, where I applied my marketing knowledge in a different context. Later, I joined another Spanish financial group and worked in Commercial Strategy before eventually relocating to Ireland, where I completed an MBA with the University of Wales, Trinity Saint David in Dublin. To further enhance my skills and continue my professional development, I am currently undertaking courses in UX Design and Software Development.

Over the past 10 years, I have embarked on an incredible journey of life in Ireland. The Irish people, their vibrant culture, and the abundant opportunities the country offers have captured my heart. During the last six years, my career at Accenture has undergone a significant transformation. I discovered that my skills were genuinely valued, and my skin colour did not hinder my success. Starting with a big tech company in Trust and Safety, I swiftly advanced to a trainer position within just six months. Two years later, I attained another promotion as a Training and Quality Lead. In this role, my team and I achieved two consecutive UKI awards, a remarkable achievement that fills me with pride. Recently, I was promoted to the position of Global Quality Lead for a different Big Tech company, overseeing teams in both Dublin and Austin, Texas, within the Legal Response Team.

Beyond my work at Accenture, I actively contribute to the African and Caribbean Network committee, where I take great pride in being an ally of the LGBTQ+ community and a supporter of the Latin America Network. Witnessing individuals like Jess Majekodunmi, a mixed-race Innovation Managing Director Lead, speaking at our 2023 International Women's Day has filled me with joy and reaffirmed my belief in the existence of opportunities for individuals of any diverse ethnic background. I wholeheartedly believe in the utmost importance of inclusion and diversity and remain committed to advocating for these values in both my personal and professional endeavours. In closing, I want to offer advice to aspiring individuals seeking a path in the tech industry. Believe in yourself and your capabilities. Embrace the privilege of being the first person with a different skin colour, ethnic background, or nationality. Use that privilege as a catalyst to open doors for others and foster a more diverse and inclusive talent pool wherever your journey takes you.

"

Believe in
yourself
& your
capabilities.

"

Scan here to learn
more about Rosa

SAMANTHA FRANCIS

EUROPEAN BENEFITS LEAD, AVANADE

Community has always been important to me. I grew up in a small military town and was one of three children of colour in school. Typically, in these environments you feel different, but I didn't and I think the fact that I was raised by parents who had a strong community of family and friends meant I always felt secure.

Culture was a big thing. Trips to Brixton market, the record shop, the Pattie shop, the barbers with my dad and the comedy videos from JA. I never felt the need to change who I was to 'fit' in. Even when they used to laugh at me at school because my hair was different. I didn't feel the need to change, but I was always very nervous when I tried a new hairstyle.

I was never particularly academic and at that time if you weren't academic, you couldn't be a success. I remember my college tutor telling me that I would be more suited to supermarket work and not the business degree I wanted to study. I spent a long time doubting myself and not trying new things because of those comments. I went from one job to another with very little purpose.

I started to think seriously about a career when I became a mother. I worked as an administrator at a large consultancy for many years and noticed that the client benefits leads were on very healthy salaries. I was intrigued because their knowledge, in most cases was not as good as mine so I decided to change career. I did my research and enrolled on a 1-year HR course. That course changed my life. I landed my first corporate job within weeks of finishing the course.

In my first role I learnt a few key things that I tell mentees. Pick companies that have a good culture and align to your moral compass. You will stay at these companies, experience greater job satisfaction, develop professionally, but importantly you will start to cultivate a community and network, that will be invaluable over the years. I have leaned on my own network many times over the years. I decided to become a mentor because I wanted to share what I have learnt and because of the years I was directionless.

The corporate space can be challenging. It's important to understand the culture, behaviour and effective communication skills, to succeed. I help mentees build these skills and discuss the different careers in technology and HR. Because the opportunities are vast, and we need more representation.

Confidence and imposter syndrome are two of the biggest professional challenges. I trained as a #IAmRemarkable facilitator to help people build their self-confidence and celebrate their achievements, as there is a tendency to diminish or minimise achievements due to bias and imposter syndrome.

Whenever I hear that voice in my head, I quieten it because I didn't get to this point by accident.

Community, network, humility, and hard work got me here.

> # Community, network, humility, & hard work got me here.

Scan here to learn more about Samantha

SANDRA ABROKWA

HEAD OF EMERGING MARKETS, STRATEGIC WEB PARTNERSHIPS, GOOGLE

The power of being last...

I am the last of 4 kids. I was the last of my friends to get into college. I was the last of my friends to get a job after college. Being the last can be hard - it can make you feel small, less-than and insecure. Sure, I was happy for my friends, and I was sure I had done my best with my applications but I couldn't help but wonder - Why didn't I get in? What am I missing? What if I don't get in anywhere? Why am I always last to do things? I can still remember the immense pressure of waiting to hear back from schools and jobs and the crushing feeling that comes with reading something akin to "we regret to inform you that..."

Yes, being the last can definitely be hard but after many years in my life and career, I have learned that being last can also be an asset and that a period of waiting to hear back on something can be a powerful time of reflection. Do you really want to do this thing that you say you want to do or when you really get to the heart of it, you're doing it because it's what's expected or because everyone else is doing it and you are afraid to be different? I was 18 years old when I first had to grapple with this - my best friend and I had always done everything together and we were preparing for college when I was waitlisted at a school she had gotten into.

I was devastated but while I waited to hear back on a final decision, I realized I didn't really want to go there - what I really wanted was to be independent and go off on my own somewhere warm and explore what life had for me. I had been afraid to admit this and it was scary to make this major step without the comfort of knowing she would be there too.

When you are forced to wait for things, you may find, like me, that waiting builds resilience and patience and the tenacity and boldness to fully grab your opportunity when it comes because you know you've really, really thought it through.

The lessons I picked up from being last and from having to wait for things have paved the way for many firsts in my professional life. It started with a bold step to move back to Ghana after 8 years living and working in the US. Many people told me I was crazy, including well-meaning friends and family. Like my college decision, I knew it was right for me. I am so glad I made that decision because it propelled me into the tech space and I have no regrets. Today, I work at Google in Dublin, and I absolutely love helping partners monetize their websites and apps and it's all because I dared to be different.

> **Waiting builds resilience, patience, tenacity & boldness.**

Scan here to learn more about Sandra

SOYINI TAYLOR

ENTERPRISE DATA ARCHITECT, SAGE

My IT journey officially started in China but the origins began before. I started out in the US enrolled in a bachelor's computer science program but failed the computer science classes freshman year. To be able to graduate on time I switched to economics which I randomly discovered but loved. Economics helped me to understand how money works and a lot of the psychology behind buying and spending at an individual (micro) and government (macro) level. I really enjoyed learning about both. With no job prospects lined up as I was about to graduate, a co-worker at my university bookstore mentioned an opportunity to teach English in China. I told my mother and aunt about it as the idea was way too far out of my comfort zone at the time. They eventually convinced me to go. I went for 6 months. It was a fascinating experience but I'd had enough of the culture shock including being followed around because I was the only black person, having my hair touched, being poked to see if I was real, etc.

Despite the culture shock of my first China trip, over time I began to miss China but I wasn't sure if I was remembering all the good (the food, culture, nightlife) and none of the bad. A few years later I decided to see how much China had changed and test the waters to see if I wanted to work there full time. I did a three-week Mandarin course at a university in Suzhou and loved every minute of it. It placed a determination within me to find my way back to China and work there full time.

While applying for masters programs, a friend referred me to a prep program planning a short-term international internship. I made sure I found my way onto the planning committee and raised the idea of going to China which they readily accepted. I became the point person for the trip by locating internship programs to be interviewed, helping finalize trip details, planning our activities, etc. During a networking event with business owners and executives, I met the person who became my boss for the next 4 years in Shanghai. When we met he said if you ever want to work in China... let me know. I went home...thought about it, reached out and the rest is history. Within months I moved to Shanghai and went to work in his food delivery company's menu editing department before transitioning to my first official IT role as a database engineer. My boss believed in me and pushed me to get a masters in IT. So I completed a bachelor's in computer science online to solidify my computer science foundation and then applied. I also became near fluent in Mandarin and volunteered at the 2010 Shanghai World Expo as a translator. This was the start of what led me to where I am now. My journey has taught me nothing is ever truly a detour.

" My journey has taught me nothing is ever truly a detour. "

Scan here to learn more about Soyini

SUNCHI CHEN

DEVELOPMENT ENGINEER, UK ATOMIC ENERGY AUTHORITY

My first name means "energy of the Sun". I consider my name a gift and, in many ways, a premonition of my life.

My father is Jamaican, whose family arrived in Britain with the Windrush generation. My mother is Bangladeshi and arrived in Britain as a war refugee. She solely raised me (the eldest daughter) and my siblings in a culturally rich community in Bristol. Many adults had described me as insatiably curious and unnervingly clever. My primary school teachers quelled my early years of self-doubt and helped to retain my innate optimism despite less fortunate circumstances. One of my fondest memories is at 8 years old where my teacher had compared me to a lotus flower. A symbol of survival, they push through dark muddy water to find light and bloom.

At adolescence, my home life and mental health became challenging. My interest in sciences took me into mostly male spaces, where I first developed imposter syndrome. Whilst my performance didn't suffer, my self-esteem crashed. I felt voiceless as my grades always overshadowed my troubles. My motive was largely to please others until a pivotal conversation with my maths teacher, who was the first woman with an engineering degree I had ever met. She told me that not only am I good enough, but better. She empowered me to trust myself with my future and to believe in my own talent. So, I decided I wanted to become an engineer, though it meant I'd self-teach some of my A-levels.

I applied to BSc Physics at the University of Birmingham but missed the grades. I felt crushed... this was my first academic failure. Though soon after, I was offered and accepted a place on their BSc Nuclear Science and Materials course instead. This ordeal became the most successful failure I've ever had. Birmingham was diverse, so I was quickly surrounded people like myself. Young, black, ambitious women. However, being the only black student on an atypical course, I still stood out. This triggered old insecurities and doubts, but I eventually accepted that I was simply not meant to blend in. I had faith that my visibility will one day serve a greater purpose to remove barriers, and therefore, remove shadows.

I found clarity after becoming a development engineer at UK Atomic Energy Authority, where I made scientific outreach a priority. I've been blessed to shine a light on vital and cutting-edge science, on myself as a black woman in the nuclear industry, and on other minorities within this space. Our mission is to lead the delivery of sustainable fusion energy and maximise its scientific and economic benefit. Fusion is the process that powers the Sun, which we want to replicate and harness for safe, low-carbon, virtually limitless energy. Energy of the Sun...my namesake. I finally feel like I'm somewhere I'm supposed to be.

If I could speak to my younger self...
You are not pretending to be smarter than you are. Everyone around believes you are talented, and soon you will believe it too.

> " Everyone around believes you are talented, soon you will believe it too. "

Scan here to learn more about Sunchi

UNETTE SPENCER

VP, CUSTOMER SOLUTIONS, MASTERCARD

When I was nine, I told my dad I wanted to be a nurse. Dad said, 'Why be a nurse when you can be a doctor?'

Dad knew lots of nurses and had huge respect for their profession, but he was encouraging me to believe in myself and to be ambitious.

My parents arrived in the UK in the 1950s and they were not welcomed. Placards and newspaper ads made it clear that Black people need not apply for jobs or housing. Mum died when I was just four, leaving Dad to care for six of us. He trained to be a Chiropodist during the day and worked night shifts at the hospital. I shared a bed with one of my sisters and the lounge carpet was threadbare, but we were loved and encouraged.

At junior school I experienced racism, and I was told to go home. But Dad had told us we had to work twice as hard as everyone else if we wanted to succeed, and I took heed. I didn't want my classmates to know about my free school meals and so I told them Dad had pre-paid for the term. By then, I was determined to have money and a nice house when I grew up.

As a sixth-form student, I cleaned Woolworths department store before school every day because there was no pocket money.

My church community friends would sometimes gently tease me for being the 'clever one,' but I didn't mind, and my sights were firmly set on university.

I loved undergraduate life, and I was excited about the opportunities my education would create. As graduation approached, I desperately wanted a job with a car, though I couldn't drive, and I couldn't afford to learn. My sister generously paid for six lessons and my boyfriend let me practice in his car, and after six months I passed.

On graduating I landed a job with Pfizer as a medical sales rep. Driving home from the training course in my blue Ford Orion I felt like a queen.

Two years later, I moved into data science and tech, initially in sales and later in consulting and leadership roles.

Dad passed twenty-three years ago, but he still inspires me and I'm so grateful for his belief and encouragement. He was right about the importance of hard work. But I learned another important lesson from someone else.

When I was in an early data science sales role, my white male boss recruited two white male guys to do the same job but at a higher grade and higher salary. When I quizzed him, he told me that they had a network of contacts that would bring new clients. As it happens, they failed and were gone within a year, but I never forgot about the importance of a network. Since then, I have consciously made connections and we provide invaluable support to one another. So, yes, work hard, but also start building your network of trusted people now.

Start building your network now.

Scan here to learn more about Unette

YEMI OLUSEUN

GROWTH & TRANSFORMATION, FINTECH

As a first-born child, I was born to lead and project manage!

I moved to the UK from Nigeria after secondary school. I struggled to integrate into the UK. Fortunately, I got access to mentors and relevant government-subsided, lifelong learning programmes. These helped me adapt, meet new people, and plug gaps in my skillset.

I credit my interest in financial inclusion and social mobility to my UK immigration experience.

I studied computer science at undergraduate and Masters level. Academically, I excelled at technical topics but knew I would not enjoy a purely technical role. Thankfully, I got the opportunity to formally start my career with JP Morgan's Graduate Programme as a Business Analyst. It turned out to be an excellent starter role. I worked with subject matter experts to elicit requirements and help create architectural models. The role helped me build my business knowledge and become an effective technologist and partner to business stakeholders. I progressed into project management roles and managed several significant transformation and expansion programmes.

One of the projects that has had the most significant impact on my career so far was working on the Barclays Ring Fencing programme. It was a regulatory programme to separate the retail business from the investment bank. It was a 2-year programme with 13 teams globally. I managed the programme from start to finish. It involved running daily calls, handling senior management reporting, learning the entire trade lifecycles of several banking products and much more. I enjoyed delivering this programme.

It helped me "fall in love" with my work and build my confidence. And I suppose it showed as I received several industry awards and recognitions for this work.

While at Barclays, I decided to complete an MBA to build my business and strategy knowledge. I studied part-time, so it required good time management skills. Thanks to the MBA, I got exposure to other industries, built my network, and travelled to work on short-term strategy projects.

After business school, I set up my own consulting business, The Change Hive. I help Financial Services businesses implement global expansion and transformation projects.

Working as a solopreneur is both rewarding and challenging. I have much more autonomy over my schedule than when I was in full-time employment. However, I now need to be more proactive about my growth. I do this by attending smaller, industry-specific events where I meet other experts and interact on a one-to-one basis. I have also been part of Masterminds, and I follow relevant podcasts & YouTube channels.

Reflecting on my experience, I have observed three groups of skills I need to work on constantly. They are clarity of my goals & mindset, commercial/ business development skills, and technical/ change management skills. Luckily, my faith, friendships, and love for learning have been good grounds for developing these. My key career learnings to date have been: Careers are marathons, not sprints, so be patient but persistent, embrace lifelong learning and be visible – speak up and advocate for yourself.

Speak up & advocate for yourself.

Scan here to learn
more about Yemi

ZULEIKA PHILIPS

HEAD OF PARTNERSHIPS & MARKETING, INTUIT

One of the hardest decisions I had to make whilst at school was deciding if I wished to wake before dawn to walk the 7 mile journey in order to pocket the £1 bus fare allocation to spend on sweets instead.

I was born into a very loving and close knit family which also unfortunately fell into the stigmatised high ratio of mixed race families in the 1980's, that of being raised by a single white mother on a council estate with my family and I being financially dependent on benefits and free school meals. My mother, who herself had been privately educated with London home in Fulham in Hurlingham Mansions and country house in Lincolnshire, left her privileged life behind when meeting my father in the 70's, beautifully embracing our African heritage, including learning how to cornrow and distracting us from our financial struggles and poverty by creating a world of imagination and ambition. When the emergency electric key would regularly run out of funds, it was not unusual to treat this as a game of hide and seek between my siblings, fill the suddenly silent house with songs from The Sound of Music and read novels by candle light or use the beam of the street lights through the windows. My mother would provoke discussions using example stories and descriptive imagery, asking us all questions to evoke meaningful goals and aspirations into our consciousness, constantly reiterating to us that we could all become whatever we wished to be and that no dream was unreachable.

My own dream was never to become one of the top 1% earners in the UK, a feat that I am proud to have achieved and have done so along with some of my siblings who also work within the STEM industry. Instead I only wished to raise a family where my children would want for nothing and would not need to put on and create brave faces at school in order to try and camouflage their home life experiences as I did. I write of my past in order to emphasize that I have always believed that it was the financial challenges from my youth that inspired and motivated the version of myself who stands on stages today and is able to do so from the natural confidence and aspirations that was instilled and nurtured environmentally from my mother and siblings.

I entered the workforce at 14yrs old delivering newspapers before school and maintained holding down part time jobs throughout my educational journey until I reached a pivotal crossroads in my early 20's. The choice in front of me was if I was going to continue down the stages of a law career or accept the offer of a full time position at a technology firm which was already putting me in the top 6% earners bracket on a part time role.

I chose the money.

I have always had an infatuation with Information Technology, its constant evolvement, new product releases, competitive platform mergers and solutions that simplify processes and behaviourisms as we react to those creations. It is a world that I cannot see myself moving away from especially when it comes to adding value and working with a company, product and team that I believe in.

The ending of any story should be the most memorable and pivotal and in this case of this book, inspiring and supportive to motivate the new emerging wave of talent from black females wishing to get into technology. You are enough.

> ## " If you possess the drive to succeed, then no dream is unreachable. "

Scan here to learn more about Zuleika

THE CARIBBEAN

Scan here to learn more about the Caribbean history

JAMAICA

Nanny of the Maroons (1686-1760)

Nanny of the Maroons was a legendary leader of the Windward Maroons, a group of escaped slaves who established a free community in the mountainous region of Jamaica in the late 17th century. Nanny was a skilled military strategist and a respected spiritual leader, known for her wisdom, courage, and resilience in the face of oppression.

GUADELOUPE

Mulatto Solitude (1772-1802)

La Mulâtresse Solitude was a legendary figure from Guadeloupe, known for her rebellion against the colonial powers in the late 18th century. She was born into slavery, but became a powerful figure in the island's slave community. While pregnant, she led a rebellion against the French colonial authorities, and her reputation as a fierce warrior and charismatic leader made her a symbol of resistance against slavery and colonialism.

HATI

Catherine Flon (1772-1831)

Catherine Flon was a Haitian seamstress who is remembered for her role in creating the first Haitian flag. She was also an enthusiastic supporter of the Haitian Revolution (1791-1804), during which she served as a nurse in a supportive capacity.

ANTIGUA & BARBUDA

Bertha Alexandrina Higgins (1889-1966)

A trailblazer for women's rights and political representation in Antigua and Barbuda. She was the first female parliamentarian in the country and a dedicated advocate for women's education and equality. Higgins was a gifted speaker and used her platform to address the challenges faced by women and girls, including poverty, domestic violence, and unequal access to education and employment.

GRENADA

Dame Hilda Bynoe (1921-2012)

She was crucial in creating the School of Arts and Sciences at St. George's University in Grenada when it was only a medical school. In addition, she was the first Grenada native and the first woman to assume the position of Governor of Grenada (1968 to 1974). She was also the first female physician to work in the interior of Guyana.

THE TECH & NON-TECH ROLES

TECH

Support Specialist: Accountable for examining and resolving computer network and hardware problems in any business.

Computer Programmer: Writes new computer software using a programming language such as HTML, CSS, JavaScript and Python.

Quality Assurance Tester: Inspects software products and makes sure they meet industry standards and have no issues.

Web Developer: Creates bespoke designs with visual content that appeals to the user and allows them to navigate web content effectively.

IT Technician: Consults with support specialists to assess and pinpoint issues with computers.

Systems Analyst: Overviews design elements and uses technical knowledge to resolve problems.

Network Engineer: Maintains and develops a company's computer network.

User Experience Designer: Uses a variety of components to develop user-friendly products that enable visual stimulation and function effectively.

Database Administrator: Organises and tracks data.

Scan to learn more about Tech roles

NON-TECH

Financial Analyst: Analyses financial data for businesses.

Sales Representative: Sells a company's products by recognising leads and educating the market on products.

Brand Specialist: Uses marketing expertise to create an easily recognisable, impactful, and unique identity for a company.

Social Media Specialist: Interacts with a business's audience to create and manage brand promotions and campaigns across multiple social media platforms.

Public Relations: Strategically communicates information to the public to build a favourable company image.

Product Manager: Monitors the success of a new product by organising multiple teams such as tech, marketing, and sales to work together efficiently.

Graphic Designer: Creates digital designs for visual identities, social media, product packaging, advertising, and print according to brand guidelines.

Copywriter: Produces written content for a variety of uses through exceptional communication skills.

Human Resources: Recruits, trains, and supports all employees within a company.

THE BLOSSOM JOURNAL

Download your free 90-day Blossom Journal to help you reflect and reframe your life to make the most of every day! This journal is a safe space for you to explore your thoughts and cultivate healthy habits of mindfulness, self-empowerment, and dreaming big. Start journaling today to get one step closer to achieving your goals like all the amazing women in this book.

PASS ON THIS BOOK NOW THAT YOU HAVE READ IT

Now that you read this book, pass it on to someone you think it will help. Discover more stories online in the extended digital edition

THE VOICES IN THE SHADOW

VOLUME 3

BY GTA BLACK WOMEN IN TECH

Scan to unlock the Digital Edition

GTA BLACK WOMEN IN TECH

Scan to learn more

GTA Black Women In Tech is a non-profit global organisation, based in London, dedicated to building bridges of opportunities in tech by enabling Black female talents to excel and companies to have access to Black women of talent. We are a community of Black women tech advocates of all levels and allies who support and empower diversity and inclusion. Our mission is to inspire, support, and connect the tech sphere to allow more Black women to excel and tech companies to perform better through diversity and inclusion.

Layout design, editing and illustration copyright © 2023 by 3 Colours Rule
(Anastasiia Yuzvak, Daniela Cardoso, Freya James, Michael Odei,
Ogechi Joseph-Anyaegbu, Yuhana Syed)
Author photos provided by the authors. Design by 3 Colours Rule.

THE VOICES IN THE SHADOW

VOLUME 3

———

By Global Tech Advocates
Black Women In Tech